Dream-work
guide to the midnight city

COMPASS OF MIND

Knowledge is a dangerous thing, as Adam and Eve found out in the Garden of Eden. Yet without it, humanity would not evolve. Knowledge leads to new pathways of understanding, shaping our views of the world and extending our ability to create. Sometimes ways in which to apply knowledge are sought; at others, knowledge itself is enough, for it is said that man is made in the image of God, and, through knowing himself, can know the divine.

The series "Compass of Mind" is founded in this view of an integrated physical, human and spiritual universe. It looks at various ways in which knowledge is discovered and formulated, drawing themes from mystical and esoteric traditions, from the creative arts, and from therapies and broad-based science. For each topic the questions are posed: "What kind of a map of the world is this?" and "What special insights does it bring?" The series title embodies the concept that knowledge begins and ends with mind; a question asked expands into a circle which is both defined and investigated by mind itself.

Authors of "Compass of Mind" titles bring a wide perspective and a depth of personal experience to their chosen themes. Each text is written with clarity and sympathy, attractive to the lay reader and specialist alike. Themes are illustrated with lively, well-researched examples, aimed at revealing the essence of the subject, for these are books which tackle the question of "Why?" rather than "How to?"

Cherry Gilchrist, series editor

DREAM-WORK

guide to the midnight city

LYN WEBSTER

DRYAD PRESS LIMITED
LONDON

*For my namesake and everyone who came
to the Thursday night dream-group.*

© Lyn Webster 1987
First published 1987
Typeset by
Progress Filmsetting Limited,
79 Leonard Street, London EC2
Printed by Biddles Ltd,
Guildford, Surrey
for the publishers
Dryad Press Limited,
8 Cavendish Square,
London W1M 0AJ

ISBN 0 8521 9733 0

CONTENTS

Acknowledgment

The cover illustration is by Gila Zur.

Chapter 1

"The Gates of Horn and Ivory"

Dreams, sir, are awkward and confusing things: not all that people see in them comes true. For there are two gates through which these insubstantial visions reach us; one is of horn and the other of ivory. Those that come through the ivory gate cheat us with empty promises that never see fulfilment; while those that issue from the gate of burnished horn inform the dreamer what will really happen. (Penelope, from Homer's *Odyssey*) (1)

Why on earth should we need to "work" on our dreams? Surely, if dreams have a function (and some people do not believe that they have), then they fulfil it anyway, whether we "work" on them or not. They sort out and digest the myriad impressions we take in every day; they fulfil our repressed wishes and punish us for long-forgotten sins; they terrify and enrapture us; they solve puzzles and set new ones; they bring the dead to life, and rub salt in old wounds; they awaken longings for impossible things and people and plunge us into thrilling erotic adventures with partners we would never consider in waking life; they change our moods for better or worse, transport us to heaven and hell – and provide us with hilarious or shocking tales to tell the mates at work. But surely they are better left alone – if not ignored, then simply endured, since they cannot be got rid of?

And more importantly, with the world in its usual parlous state, surely it is not good for people to turn inward and explore the contents of their unconscious minds, when it would be more useful if they spent their time and energy trying to make the "real" world a better place!

That seemed to me a quite persuasive line of argument, until I considered this: how can we learn to control the negative and destructive forces in the world if we cannot even understand, never mind control, those forces within ourselves? If, as individuals, we are all at the mercy of drives within us that we cannot command ("I don't know what came over me", "I can't help it", "Something snapped and I just hit him"), what makes us think we have any chance of changing the external world for the better?

On the other hand, if we were able to chart some of that vast, unexplored area within us which we call the "unconscious", might we not be able to put that knowledge to good use? And if, as Freud thought, dreams are the "royal road to the unconscious", do they not offer us the most marvellous opportunity to turn the beam of our consciousness onto the dark, hidden things of the human psyche, and perhaps make discoveries which could change the course of our personal histories – and who knows, the history of our planet too?

Large claims? Ah, but I'm a dreamer, and so are you, or you wouldn't be reading this book! We explorers of the inner realms, pioneers, adventurers in dream-time and dream-space, will never be the public heroes that mountaineers or astronauts can be, but our job is just as important, though unsung and unreported. And there are dangers and pitfalls in this inner world just as in the outer – and so, before we set off on our travels, I would like to devote this first chapter to considering what they are. Don't let us fall prey to the kind of silliness and woolly-mindedness which often afflict people when they step out of the familiar into the mysterious. Let us arm ourselves with a clarity of vision and purpose which will hold us steady when everything around us is changing shape and shifting ground, as everything tends to do in the dream-world.

What, then, are the problems and perils we encounter while working with dreams? The biggest one is that dreams themselves are such tricksy and treacherous phenomena: it is very difficult to understand what our dreams mean because we are usually biassed by what we *want* them to mean. Therefore, even if they are telling us the truth (and they do not always do so – dreams can lie), we may not be ready to accept that truth, and prefer to misinterpret the dream accordingly. It is no accident that the god who brings us dreams is Hermes/Mercury, for although he is both the psychopomp (guide of the soul) and messenger of the gods who can lead you to the truth, he is also the trickster who can lead you up the garden path! Here is an example of what I mean.

Maria (a good friend of mine) was in love with a handsome and brilliant man. He was friendly towards her, but did not seem to return her love. She dreamed she was at a party, wandering from room to room, looking for him, but she could not find him and eventually sat down in despair. At this point he appeared, knelt down and laid his head in her lap. "Why are you so difficult to find?" he asked.

Naturally enough Maria was cheered by this dream: she felt sure that it was telling her that the man really did love her, but that she should stop chasing him and wait for him to come to her. She did so, but he did not come! She was disappointed and puzzled, but as she recovered from her fruitless infatuation, she examined the dream's symbolism more closely: her beloved had laid his head in her lap just like the unicorn in the old myths, and she did indeed think of him as a rare and magical being, just as the unicorn is a rare and magical beast. But, as she remembered, the unicorn who gives himself up in this way is then caught and slain by the hunters. The maiden who attracts him is there to lure him to his death. Could it be that the man loved her but was frightened of her, frightened that if he allowed himself to be drawn towards her she would destroy him? Thinking of his ambivalent behaviour towards her, she recognised that this was probably true, and took it to be the "message" of the dream.

Some time later, when she had completely recovered from her obsession and was in love with someone else, she met him again. He revealed that he had indeed been very drawn towards her, but at the same time frightened and repelled by her intense and demanding demeanour. "But now you're so different," he said, "so calm and serene . . . "

She realised that the relationship she had longed for would be possible now, but she no longer wanted it! She was still "difficult to find".

So the dream had told her the "truth", but in a form which she was unable to make sense of at the time. And by the time she had grown up and developed enough to understand it, its "message" was not of much use to her. And yet . . . maybe the dream had precipitated the process of change which had liberated her from her obsession . . . or maybe the real function of the dream was to herald this healing process, not to give her a comforting reassurance that "he really does love you deep down after all". Dreams do not follow the logic of our waking minds, and the dream-worker has to take this into account when she or he looks for "results". They come all right, but usually not in the form you expect.

Another example: a young man in our dream-group used to dream from time to time of a girl he had known at school – she had, he said, a spiritual quality about her and had once intended to become a nun. Then one night he awoke at five o'clock, with a vivid sense that this girl was in some sort of trouble, and a complete telephone number in his mind. He was so stirred by the dream that he jumped out of bed and dialled the number. Eventually a Scottish voice answered. "Is Helen there?" he asked boldly. "She is *not*." "Is that Blackpool?" (She had lived in Blackpool.) "It is *not* – it is Aberdeen! And it is five o'clock in the morning . . . " He hung up of course and went back to bed.

Just a funny story, evidence that we shouldn't take dreams too seriously? Or did the girl represent some part of that young man with which he urgently needed to get in touch? Or maybe she *was* in trouble, but not on the end of that particular telephone line. Or perhaps the number he 'phoned was a convent, and Helen *had* become a nun and changed her name . . . . We will never know because when he woke again he had forgotten the number.

I have deliberately chosen two odd, unsatisfactory examples to make a point about the difficulty of knowing what dreams *really* mean – or indeed if they mean anything at all. It is because of the tricksiness of dreams that in all societies where dream-work has been done, great care has been taken to prepare those who do the work, to train their powers of discrimination and insight, so that they will not be fooled by the false trails of dreams coming through the "gates of ivory", or indeed by delusions of their own making. In certain tribal cultures dreams are handled by shamans who have been trained by means of gruelling initiations until they are utterly at home in the dream-world and know its rules back to front – even to the extent, in some cases, of having dream-wives and dream-children! In ancient Greece those who wished to have a healing dream in the temple had to fast and bathe and purify themselves before entering the precincts. Psychoanalysts must submit to analysis themselves before they may analyse other people's dreams – and in a properly run dream-group the leader will have explored her own dreams very thoroughly before she attempts to show others how to work with theirs.

The second big problem for the dream-worker is that the conscious and the unconscious mind do not share a language: the waking mind is inclined to dismiss the products of the dreaming mind as "nonsense", while the dreaming mind breaks all the basic structural rules by which the waking mind builds its world. It is as if the mind were a dark globe and our waking consciousness a little illuminated spot on it, our "home-base". While we sleep that light goes out and a searchlight sweeps randomly around the dark parts of the globe (the "unconscious"), feeding images back like an outside broadcast camera to the control-room at home-base, where they are recorded and reviewed in the morning. The problem is that the "day-shift" workers who watch the recordings find it difficult to make sense of the picture sequences which the "night-shift" cameramen have taken. They are used to watching nicely directed and edited programmes and are baffled by the weird, random montages of imagery which the enthusiastic but undisciplined night-workers have produced.

How then can the day-shift make sense of the night-shift's work? And how can the night-shift help the day-shift understand what they see? This is the problem which dream-workers face: how to make a relationship between the conscious and the unconscious mind which is beneficial to both – so that the consciousness has a much wider field of perception and the unconscious becomes organised to some degree.

It sounds simple but it is not. As C.G. Jung wrote, "becoming conscious is of course a sacrilege against nature, it is as though you had robbed the unconscious of something." (2) In other words, the unconscious is not easily robbed of its secrets and will try to make the robber pay for what he takes in some way. By working on dreams we attempt to "pay" in terms of effort and clarity, so that we do not have to "pay" in some other way (which might be more painful). But it is interesting that Jung used the word "robbed", because it reminds me of the myth of Prometheus, the heroic Titan (half-man, half-god) who stole the secret of fire from the gods, to give it to mankind. In fact, Prometheus is a good hero for dream-workers because he was someone who could move both in the visible world (the world of men) and in the invisible world (the realm of the gods, the unconscious), and who had the courage and the cunning to steal what was valuable from the unconscious and bring it up into the conscious mind. Some people would say that his fire was a symbol of consciousness itself, in which case the myth is even more relevant to us since the dream-worker is trying to become more conscious all the time, to shine a light into the dark world of dreams.

You can see that, because of these problems, it is easy to get nowhere at all with the business of understanding your dreams. Even if you decide to be systematic about it, there are so many systems to choose from, each with its own bias, that it is easy to give up in confusion. The Freudians analyse dreams to find complexes, usually with sexual secrets at their core; Jungians use dream-work to accelerate the process of "individuation" via the archetypal images which surface in dreams; while modern dream-workers often incorporate psychological techniques from the world of "personal growth" to bring about change and expansion of the personality. Then of course there are scientists who will tell you that dreaming is simply the brain's activity as an "off-line" computer, sorting and cataloguing impressions from the previous day. And there are many other individuals with intriguing theories of their own which they will be happy to impose on you.

In this book I hope to give you a taste of as many of these different ways of working with dreams as possible, but first, in order to help us find our way through the labyrinth, I am going to stick my neck out and offer my own chart of this disputed territory. It is based simply on my own observations and discussions with other dream-workers, and I present it only as a rough guide which you can discard as soon as you have found something better of your own.

The chart is a very simple one: six different categories of dreams, each one belonging to a different level of being, starting with the most physical, instinctive level and climbing up to the most spiritual.

At the bottom of the chart we have the most basic sort of

dream, the kind which fulfils a primary *instinctive* need: for example, if you are actually hungry or thirsty in your sleep, you may dream of eating or drinking; if you need to empty your bladder you may dream of doing so (and of course small children sometimes actually do it!) and if you are sexually frustrated you may dream of making love and having an orgasm. Such dreams do not really need to be worked on, although they may tell you something useful about your state of being, and of course they may just be a small part of a richer, more meaningful dream.

At the next level up we find *digestive* dreams. These are the sort of dreams which run through the impressions of the previous day and sort them into categories for storage and remembering. Thus you may find yourself dreaming of a girl you were at school with, and, if you follow the chain of associations which lead from her, you will remember that the doctor who examined you that day had the same high-pitched laugh as she did, or the same name, and this is the mind's way of finding a place for the new impression in the library of your memory. Such dreams are often remembered as disconnected fragments.

Next come *balancing* and *integrative* dreams, and these are the dreams in which we dramatise and struggle with the psychological or emotional conflicts of our life at the time. This is where useful dream-work can really begin. As soon as you start to keep a dream diary you will be able to observe how this sort of dream mirrors what is happening to you in vivid and telling imagery. Thus while I was involved in a draining and pointless relationship I dreamed of a tree standing in a pot. When I pulled it out, I saw that it had no roots and wondered how it had survived. But then, in the dream-work I did later, I saw the tree burst its pot and stretch its roots out into the rich soil. From this I understood that the relationship had been constricting me, stopping me from growing. I ended it soon afterwards.

Most of the interesting dreams we have come from this

level, but beyond it lie the real treasures of dreaming. One rung up we find *creative* dreaming: here is where the *new* can enter in, where artists find inspiration, thinkers solutions to apparently insoluble problems, and where we all occasionally experience the kind of inventive, thrilling or hilarious dreams which make us wonder at the mind's hidden powers. These dreams often have a satisfying *structure* not found in the more common fragmentary dreams. They may well even tell a story with a beginning, a middle and an end.

Next comes *true-dreaming*, which covers precognitive, clairvoyant and prophetic dreaming. Here the dreamer "sees" what is true, not just in a psychological sense but also in a concrete, physical sense. Thus a woman might dream that her son is ill, and find out the next day that he is in hospital after a heart-attack. In cases like this, the barrier between the waking and the dreaming worlds seems momentarily to dissolve. However, these dreams are very rare.

Lastly we come to those *"big" dreams* which shake the foundations of a person's life, usually for the better. Here there is definitely a sense that the dream is coming from a higher part of ourselves, expressing wisdom or knowledge not normally accessible to us. Jacob's dream of the ladder reaching up to heaven comes in this category, as would those very rare dreams from which we wake dazzled, shaken or profoundly moved, which stay with us for years, if not for life.

Of course it is quite possible that one dream will contain dreaming from more than one level, and you may well have dreams which don't fit into these categories neatly. The point of this structure is not to slap labels on experience, but to *organise* our minds in preparation for investigative work: not all dreams are equally worth working on and there is no point in wasting time pondering on the meaning of the currant bun you ate in a dream last night if you went to bed hungry having eaten currant buns for tea! Similarly, some "big" dreams do not need interpretation, and you might lose something of their power in your life if you worry away at them instead of just letting them float in your mind, and impart their meaning in their own way.

However, since this book is about *dream-work* – not *dreaming* – I am going to build it around different sorts of dream-work rather than different sorts of dream. I will start by looking at the long tradition of *therapeutic dream-work* – the noble idea that dreams can be used to heal. Then I shall move on to consider dream-work as a tool for *self-development*, and further, as a means of contacting the *creative* within us. Then we will explore the fascinating phenomena of *lucid-dreaming* – when you are dreaming and *know* that you are dreaming – and *true-dreaming*, which raises some mind-stretching philosophical and metaphysical issues. Finally we will look at those *"big" dreams* which seem to come from a higher power either inside or outside ourselves.

The examples of dreams and dream-work which I will be giving in the book come either from already published sources, or from my own experience and that of friends and fellow-dream-workers. In every case I have asked permission of the dreamer before quoting his or her dream – a dream is after all a very private and personal affair.

I will not be telling you about the physiology of dreaming (REM sleep etc), neither will I be presenting you with a linear historical survey of work on dreams, with great chunks embedded in it giving you everything you need to know about Freud or Jung. There are already plenty of books which do those things. Rather I offer a series of essays, each on a different aspect of dream-work, written with the objective of stimulating you and inspiring you to do your own dream-work, as well as informing you about the work others have done. And since dream-work requires a fine balance between self-discipline and free imagination you will find that the tone of these essays reflects that and alternates between the rational and the lyrical, the impersonal and the personal, the abstract and the down-to-earth. And I must come clean and say that I don't write this book as a scientist or a psychologist, but as a writer (a novelist to be exact) and a life-long explorer of the land of dreams: I have recorded my dreams for nearly twenty years, run dream-groups and workshops and tried out personally most of the techniques mentioned in this book. I believe that dreams are meaningful, but I have found that the study of dreams and the practice of dream-work offer no easy solutions to problems, no effortless creativity, no short-cuts to enlightenment. In fact, unless you already possess the ability to look at yourself with honesty, then it might be better not to start at all because, for someone really attached to their illusions, dream-work offers magnificent opportunities for continued self-deception and inflation of the ego!

To my mind, the final test of dream-work must always be: does it make me more alert, more alive, more connected in my waking life? If not, beware, because the mental hospitals are full of dreamers who have dreamed up their own worlds, and now live in them alone, quite cut off from our common reality. Dream-work is not an escape from life, but a coming to terms with it, all of it – the good and the bad. And, paradoxically, if you would learn to dream properly, you must first learn how to wake up . . .

Chapter 2

Healing with Dreams: The Masters

The alternative to recalling and interpreting dreams is not always pleasant. Individuals cannot expect to drift forever. If they do not puzzle out their identity and the direction of their lives by the aid of their dreams (which, he said, every normal person should try to do), then they may be brought, by the relentless action of their pent-up souls, into some crisis which requires that they come to terms with themselves. It may be a medical crisis. It may be the end of a marriage or of a job. It may be depression or withdrawal. (Harmon Bro, from *Edgar Cayce on Dreams*) (3)

We have all had the experience of waking up in the morning, after going to bed troubled or anxious, to find ourselves in a quite different mood – positive, hopeful, fizzing with energy – and of watching how this new mood dissolves the obstacles which loomed so ominously the day before. Something has happened in the night. Our dreams have sorted things out, organised our energy, set a new direction. In other words, a healing process has been in action.

We may or may not remember what the dreams were. It doesn't matter – they have done their work. But, for most of us, this magical renewal does not happen often enough. Sometimes we wake up feeling worse than when we went to bed. Or perhaps our problems are too serious to be solved by a good night's sleep. Maybe we have a chronic physical illness. Maybe we are psychologically crippled to such an extent that life has become a prisonhouse.

I would bet that, as long as man has been conscious of the difference between sleeping and waking, he has hoped that dreams might contain a secret remedy for his ills and grievances. We sense that the dreaming mind has access to bits of the jig-saw which the conscious mind cannot find. If only we could make a net to catch the magical fish who swim in the murky depths of sleep! Then we would be cured, then we would become the radiant, happy human beings we were always meant to be! But how do we do it? Dreams are so opaque, so absurd, often so inconsequential. How can we unlock their healing power?

One of the first problems we face, as psychotherapist Arnold Mindell puts it, is that "the unconscious does not know how to communicate to consciousness, partially from the fact that the conscious mind listens to nothing but itself." (4) However, there is one very simple way in which the conscious mind can show its willingness at least to listen to the unconscious: by keeping a dream diary. Even without any particular knowledge of dream theories or interpretation, anyone who does this regularly over a period of time will notice certain themes and symbols recurring in his or her dreams. These will indicate what the main psychological conflicts are at that time. In other words, they can be used as a means of diagnosis.

For instance, before I began to study dreams seriously, I kept a record of them in my diary, and I could not fail to notice that one of my favourite themes was that there was a swimming-pool or lake which I wanted to jump into, but could not. Either it was too dirty, maybe clogged with weeds which would wrap around my legs if I ventured in, or the entrance price was too high, or there was not enough time – I had to be somewhere else. It did not require much in the way of interpretative skills for me to work out that the pool was symbolic of the world of emotion, and that I was afraid of that world. I feared that, if I plunged into it, I would be dragged down, contaminated, have to pay a stiff price, use up all my time and energy, etc, etc. So, these dreams showed me what was *wrong*, but not how to put it *right*.

Similarly Sarah, a member of the dream-group, reported this as a recurring dream:

I am feeling happy, relaxed and confident. I am dressed well and I am amongst friends at some sort of party. All of a sudden I am faced with a BUFFET. I start with a little plate, picking up bits of celery, bread and so on. Then, all of a sudden, I eat one thing too many and my control is GONE! I eat everything – pieces of pie, quiche, trifle. . . . My friends are blotted out, everything is blotted out. All that exists is the frenzy of eating. I wake in a sweat, but am very relieved that I haven't really got all that lot on board!

Again, it is not difficult to discern what this dream is saying. At the simplest level it is telling Sarah that she has an eating problem (which is true); at a more complex level it is expressing her anxieties about accepting love. Because she had a loveless childhood she has no in-built sense of balance about how much love (food) she needs to receive (eat) and fears, more than anything, that she might "go out of control". The problem is very clearly depicted in the dream, but what action can Sarah take to solve it? Does the dream contain the seed of a solution?

In fact, without the mediation of somebody experienced in dream-work, it is very difficult to go further than diagnosis, to unlock the healing function, for the reason that the ego or waking mind will probably have strong resistances to accepting the clues which the dreaming mind has thrown up. In order to be healed (made whole), the dreamer would have to let go of what she is and allow a transformation to begin. But the ego does not want to change. Its function is to maintain the status quo, the integrity of the individual. So, although the dreamer knows what is wrong with her, she is paralysed by a reluctance to do anything about it.

It is therefore not surprising that most therapeutic dream-work is concerned with ways of circumventing the ego's objections to change, so that the person is able to take action and heal him or herself. This sounds easy but it is not. Even if we do not like what we are, it is a known, safe, familiar quantity to us: to change is to step into the unknown, and that usually feels dangerous and undesirable. Illness or neurosis, although unpleasant, always represent a *solution* to a problem or conflict. If we dissolve our illness, we lose our solution and have to find another – which may mean facing up to a conflict we wanted to ignore and have buried in our illness.

One of the oldest techniques for solving this problem was (and still is) dream *incubation*. This meant asking the God of Dreams for a special dream which would tell you what to do to heal yourself. But before you could hope to have this dream you had to prepare yourself carefully: in some cultures you would fast or pray or isolate yourself; in others you might place certain herbs under your pillow or wrap yourself in the skin of a sacrificial animal; or you might go to a sacred place dedicated to dreams – a dream temple or a chasm supposed to be the entrance to the underworld.

The result of these practices was to jolt you out of the everyday world, shift you up from the usual ego level to a higher level of consciousness, and thereby open the mind to knowledge of a different order.

Dream incubation was very widespread in the ancient world. We know that the Egyptians, Greeks and Celts all practised it in their different ways. However, the best written evidence on the results of incubation rites comes to us from the fifth century, when there was a resurgence of interest in the cult of Asklepios in Greece. The Epidaurian temple records, discovered and published in the nineteenth century, plus the writings of Aristides on the subject, show us that the suppliant actually expected to *see* the divine healer Asklepios in his dream, and to receive specific instructions from him. Some of the remedies reported seem sensible – gargling for a sore throat or eating vegetables for constipation. Others are magical, such as the instruction to smear the eyes with the blood of a white cock, and some sound downright painful! To cure various complaints, Aristides was instructed to take powerful emetics, go river-bathing in winter, get ship-wrecked and sacrifice a finger! And yet Aristides had great faith in the process. He gives us this account of his encounter with the god:

It was like seeming to touch him, a kind of awareness that he was there in person; one was between sleeping and waking, one wanted to open one's eyes and yet was anxious lest he should withdraw too soon; one listened and heard things, sometimes as in a dream, sometimes as in waking life; one's hair stood on end; one cried and felt happy; one's heart swelled but not with vainglory . . . (5)

But the Greek scholar E.R. Dodds, who is the collector of all this information, is sceptical about the efficacy of the incubation method. Is there much to be said, he asks, "for a system which placed the patient at the mercy of his own unconscious impulses?" Dodds suggests that Aristides had a repressed desire to be punished, which the painful dream remedies satisfied. And although the record of contented suppliants tells us that incubation did work at least some of the time (I suppose the discontented were not asked to write down their complaints!), there is obviously a real danger that incubated dreams might simply provide material to feed neurosis and illness rather than cure them.

In classical times, Hippocrates, the father of medicine, tried to rationalise the interpretation of dreams for diagnostic purposes by deciding on a table of correspondances between dream-symbols and parts of the body. Thus earth in a dream represented flesh, rivers blood, and so on. Combined with good medical skills and developed powers of observation, no doubt this system was useful, but it doesn't address itself to the basic problem: how to translate the messages of the unconscious into a form which the conscious mind can assimilate and use.

This is where the shaman comes in. In many cultures, particularly in Siberia, North America and Japan, he or she has been (and in some cases still is) the mediator between the dreaming and waking worlds, who brings healing to his tribe.

But before he can do the job he must undergo rigorous and lengthy training. This will begin when he is "called" to his vocation either by a grave illness or by a special dream, or both. He will then be subjected to a period of isolation, starvation or physical suffering, or a combination of these ordeals, designed to destroy the conditioning which gives him an ordinary human sense of self and to put him in touch with the titanic energies which play in the unconscious.

In her book on Japanese shamanism Carmen Blacker explains the process:

By breaking down the ordinary human habits of living, by drastically altering the rhythms of sleep and eating, and above all by subjecting the body to extreme degrees of cold, the system is reduced to a point where mere collapse would usually ensue. Where the sacred world lies before one, however, these stresses become the means of opening a crack or vent in the hard carapace of human habit, enabling a new source of power to stream in. (6)

Once this change has taken place there follows a series of extraordinary experiences which the shaman undergoes while in a kind of waking dream or trance. Mircea Eliade gives an account of one variety of initiation among the Yakuts:

. . . the evil spirits carry the future shaman's soul to the underworld and there shut it up in a house for three years. Here the shaman undergoes his initiation. The spirits cut off his head, which they set aside (for the candidate must watch his own dismemberment with his own eyes) and cut him into small pieces, which are then distributed to the spirits of various diseases. Only by undergoing such an ordeal will the future shaman gain the power to cure. His bones are then covered with new flesh, and in some cases he is also given new blood. (7)

The ordeal of being cut into pieces or dismembered (in the dream-world!) is common to most shamanic initiations, and after it, the shaman can transform himself into an animal or bird or any other shape necessary for his operations in the "otherworld". In fact he can enter and leave that world at will to bring back knowledge for the tribe. He *organises* that chaotic world by effort of will and can extract meaning from it which is inaccessible to an uninitiated person.

Many primitive peoples believe that illness is caused by "loss of soul". So, when a healing séance is held, the shaman undertakes to make a journey into the "otherworld" or underworld to search for the soul of the sick person and bring it back. From his own experiences there, he is familiar with its geography, rules and dangers.

The séance often takes the form of a ritual: a symbolic journey is enacted which mirrors the inner journey being made by the shaman. He may communicate his adventures to the others present by singing or reciting, as they wait anxiously to know if his efforts have been successful. Eliade tells how, in one tribe, if the shaman finds that the Lord of Death is particularly reluctant to relinquish a soul, it may be necessary for him to arrange an exchange or sacrifice in order to win it back. Then, with the patient's agreement, he will pick a victim and, changing himself into an eagle, swoop down and steal that poor man's soul. He will then present it to the Lord of Death in exchange for his patient's soul. Presumably the de-souled victim then dies instead of the patient!

But what, you may ask, have these esoteric activities to do with the kind of dream-work we might do in suburban Manchester or London? The answer lies in the parallel between the shaman's magical operations in the "otherworld" and what goes on in dreams. In shamanic magic a symbolic ritual is performed to show the people in the séance the changes that are being effected in the unconscious world. If the shaman's magic works, then those changes will actually happen in the physical and the psychological worlds, as well as in the unconscious, because *the symbols he uses have meaning at every level*. In dreams, symbols with deep personal and/or collective meaning are played with and tried out in various patterns, but usually there is no change in the waking life because the dreamer does not *remember* his dream, or if he does, does not attempt to *understand* its symbolic meaning. To put it simply, in *magic* a conscious will is at work in the unconscious realm, while in *dreams* there is usually no ordering will, no "director". This is where dream-work comes in and borrows some techniques from magic. Via dream-work we can learn to bring our conscious will to bear on the unconscious, to understand its language, to organise it a little, and perhaps eventually we may win some power to direct what happens there.

Now, to obtain this power, the shaman abandons his ego, his day-to-day self, and makes another more flexible vehicle for his being. It is obviously not advisable (even if it were possible!) for us to undergo a voluntary death of the ego in order to penetrate the world of dreams! The contemporary western way is altogether more cautious and intellectual . . .

Carl Jung might have been pleased to be called a shaman, but Sigmund Freud would probably have been insulted by the title. And yet, in a sense, that is what these two great, innovative healers were – shamans. They both recognised the need to pass through the fire themselves before they could subject anyone else to its healing flames. Jung undertook a lonely journey into the depths of his own unconscious, in which he encountered all sorts of archetypal beings, and strayed very close to the borders of sanity. Freud submitted himself to a rigorous self-analysis, in which he had to face many unpleasant aspects of himself and let go of many cherished illusions. While perhaps not quite as harrowing as the shaman's ritual dismemberment, these initiations certainly gave the two men access to knowledge which no-one had seriously contemplated before, and for each dreams were central.

It was while he was engaged in his self-analysis that

Freud was writing *The Interpretation of Dreams*, and he used many of his own dreams (sometimes severely censored) as illustrations in the book. It has therefore the kind of passion which comes when a man is struggling to attain not only objective truth but also the truth about himself. Although it was slated at the time, it eventually became enormously influential, and Freud himself thought of it as his masterpiece.

How did Freud use dreams in his therapeutic practice? At the core of his philosophy was the idea that dreams are *always* an attempt at wish-fulfilment, even if the wishes are long-repressed and denied. He believed that these wishes often had their roots in infantile experience; therefore themes like the Oedipus complex (love for parent of the opposite sex and jealousy of the parent of the same sex) could be expected to crop up, in disguised form, in people's dreams. Freud also did a great deal of work decoding the *language* of dreams: he showed for instance how many associations and meanings can be *condensed* into one word or one symbol, thereby discovering that free-association from this word or symbol will lead you eventually to the core of a patient's neurosis. This is one of the examples he gives:

One of my women patients told me a short dream which ended in a meaningless verbal compound. She dreamt she was with her husband at a peasant festivity and said: 'This will be a general "Maistollmutz" '. In the dream she had the vague sort of feeling that it was some kind of pudding made with maize – a sort of polenta. Analysis divided the word into 'mais' ('maize'), 'toll' ('mad'), 'mannstoll' ('nymphomaniac') and 'Olmutz' (a town in Moravia). All these fragments were found to be remnants of a conversation she had had at table with her relatives. The following words lay behind 'mais': 'Meissen' (a Meissen (Dresden) porcelain figure representing a bird); 'Miss' (her relative's English governess had just gone to Olmutz); and 'mies' (a Jewish slang word used to mean 'disgusting'). A long chain of thoughts and associations led off from each symbol in this verbal hotchpotch. (8)

Freud does not tell us what this lady's neurosis was, but perhaps from the nature of the associations emerging from this analysis we can guess!

Freud uncovered many of the tricks of the dreaming mind: *displacement*, for instance, where the essence of the dream is replaced by some other material because that essence is unacceptable to the conscious mind: you might have an apparently innocent dream about a holiday at the seaside with your wife, but analysis would show that the name of the hotel is strangely similar to that of your sister-in-law, and you might then admit that you were attracted to your sister-in-law and that the dream was really about your desire to commit adultery with her. . . . Related to this is the use of what Freud called the dream *censor* to hide the unpalatable identity of things behind more acceptable symbols – for example, a hat appearing as a symbol of the male genitals.

In *The Interpretation of Dreams* he quotes fascinating work by Herbert Silberer, who was curious about the way in which thoughts were transformed into pictures in dreams. To watch this process Silberer set himself a series of intellectual tasks while in a sleepy, fatigued condition. Here are a couple of examples:

Example 1 – I thought of having to revise an uneven passage in an essay.
Symbol – I saw myself planing a piece of wood.
Example 2 – I had lost the thread in a train of thought. I tried to find it again, but had to admit that the starting point had completely escaped me.
Symbol – Part of a compositor's forme, with the last lines of type fallen away. (9)

Of course, in dream interpretation we have to work the other way round, from the picture to the thought. But if you try Silberer's experiment yourself you will gain insight into your own image-making mechanism, and this may help you in interpreting your dreams.

From his years of analytic work with patients Freud observed that certain common dream symbols seemed to mean the same thing in different patients' dreams. The meanings were usually sexual.

All elongated objects, such as sticks, tree-trunks and umbrellas (the opening of these last being comparable to an erection) may stand for the male organ. . . . Boxes, cases, chests, cupboards and ovens represent the uterus. . . . Steps, ladders or staircases, or, as the case may be, walking up or down them, are representations of the sexual act. (10)

Even if we consider that Freud's detective-work on symbolism too often led him to sex, we have to admire his decoding skills! Possibly in the Vienna of the early twentieth century there was a degree of sexual repression amongst the bourgeoisie which made them more subconsciously obsessed with sex than we are, in our "liberated" times. On the other hand, maybe he was right: maybe sex does lie at the bottom of most things. (Oops, a horrible Freudian pun!)

When he was analysing a patient's dream Freud would basically try to unpack and unpick it, drawing out all the associations, unmasking symbols, looking for any trails leading to repressed material, in the hope that the insight gained by the patient into her condition would serve to free her from it. We have no way of knowing whether Freud's interpretations of his patients' dreams were always correct, but it is easy to see how the introduction of order and meaning into the chaotic and apparently absurd world of the dream could have a liberating and therapeutic effect, even if the actual interpretation were wrong.

To give a flavour of Freud's methods, here is the story of a woman patient who dreamed she saw her fifteen-year-old daughter lying dead "in a case". The woman just could not see how this could be construed as a wish-fulfilment dream. However, during the course of the analysis, she remembered that at a party the night before she had been having a discussion about all the different words which could be used to translate the English word "box" – amongst them "Schachtel", the German for "case". She then recalled guessing that the German word "Büchse" (receptacle) must be related to the English "box", and that "Büchse" was a slang word for the female genitals. . . . Could the daughter in the "case" be a representation of an embryo in the womb? Now the dream's meaning became clear: fifteen years ago, when she had become pregnant, she had bitterly resented the fact, and, in a violent scene with her husband, had beaten her stomach with her fists, as if to kill the foetus. So the dream *did* embody a wish-fulfilment, but the wish was an old, out-dated one, perhaps revived in her unconscious by some present guilty feeling towards her daughter. (11)

Some of the most impressive interpretations in the book are of Freud's own dreams, and they demonstrate the unflinching honesty of his approach. One of these dreams had a particularly unpleasant content:

A hill, on which there was something like an open-air closet: a very long seat with a large hole at the end of it. Its back edge was thickly covered with small heaps of faeces of all sizes and degrees of freshness. There were bushes behind the seat. I micturated on the seat; a long stream of urine washed everything clean; the lumps of faeces came away easily and fell into the opening. It was as though at the end there was still some left. (12)

He doesn't waste time feeling revolted with himself for producing such imagery, but asks "Why did I feel no disgust during this dream?" He then proceeds to uncover a whole series of *positive* associations: "the Augean stables which were cleansed by Hercules. This Hercules was I"; the location of the dream in a place which looked like Aussee where he "had discovered the infantile aetiology* of the neuroses and had thus saved my own children from falling ill". Even the stream of urine which washes everything clean he recognised as "an unmistakable sign of greatness" because it was in that way that Gulliver put out the great fire of Lilliput, and thus that Rabelais' superman Gargantua revenged himself on the Parisians (he sat on

*infant aetiology: originating in early childhood.

Notre Dame and turned his stream of urine upon the city!) (13)

Thus Freud detected his own egotism and accepted it. A lesser man would not have done that. And we must follow his brave example if we are to get at the often unpalatable truth of our dreams . . .

Jung was for a long time a friend and disciple of Freud, immensely excited and impressed by his theory of dreams. But eventually disagreements emerged. From his own experience of working with patients' dreams Jung felt there was more to them than wish-fulfilment. He thought that what his patients were longing for was not so much the satisfaction of an often erotic wish as the achievement of a kind of psychic balance or wholeness, even, in some cases, a connection with the divine.

One of the first signs of this divergence appears in a letter from Jung to Freud dated 8 May 1911:

At the moment I am looking into astrology, which seems indispensable for a proper understanding of mythology. There are strange and wondrous things in these lands of darkness. Please don't worry about my wanderings in these infinitudes. I shall return laden with rich booty for our knowledge of the human psyche. For a while longer I must intoxicate myself on magic perfumes in order to fathom the secrets that lie hidden in the abysses of the unconscious. (14)

Two years later Jung strikes the final blow, as he explains where he now stands on dreams:

We fully admit the soundness of the wish-fulfilment theory, but we maintain that this way of interpreting dreams touches only the surface, that it stops at the symbol, and that further interpretation is possible. When, for instance, a coitus wish appears in a dream, this wish can be analysed further, since this archaic expression of its tiresome monotony of meaning needs retranslating into another medium. We recognise the soundness of the wish-fulfilment theory up to a certain point, but we go beyond it. In our view it does not exhaust the meaning of dreams. (15)

Freud never replied to this letter.

Jung, like Freud, thought of himself as a scientist, but he

did not shut anything out of the scope of his researches. He investigated world mythology, archeology, alchemy; he visited primitive tribes; he considered the principles and practice of all the great religions. From his wide studies he came to the conclusion that there were certain themes and symbols which appeared in the myths and dreams of men all over the world, and posited that this "collective unconscious" represented a unified strata deep in the psyche of mankind. This idea provided a depth and a structure to his interpretations of dreams which gave him the confidence to use work on dreams as a means of *transformation*, both for himself and for his patients.

This is a different order of healing from that practised by Freud. The individual is not simply returned to normal; he or she is opened up to the possibility of contacting the great archetypes which stand in the borderland between the known and the unknown world. A person who does this will, according to Jung, begin to operate differently: no longer confined within the narrow limits of the ego, harassed by anxiety and neurosis, but liberated into a bigger, richer world fed from the true source of life, the "Self". (By the "Self" Jung does not mean the "self" as we would use the word, but something very like God.)

In fact, as he grew older Jung relied less and less upon strict psychoanalytical method and allowed his intuition more free play. He gives a wonderful example of how he used *his own dreams* to heal, in an unusual psychoanalytical relationship.

He dreamed that a young woman came to him as a patient and explained her case to him. But he did not understand what she was saying at all and could only think that she must have a most unusual father complex. The dream meant little to him at the time, but the next day a young Jewish woman came to him for treatment of a severe anxiety neurosis. At first he was perplexed, but then he remembered his dream and realised "this is the woman of my dream!" However, he could find no trace of father complex in her, and finally resorted to asking about her grandfather. It turned out that he had been a "zaddick" (a saintly rabbi) in the mystical sect of Chassidim. Jung suggested to the girl that, although her father had turned away from his faith, she was not finding it possible to do the same.

"You have your neurosis because the fear of God has got into you," he told her, and he reports that his suggestion "struck her like a bolt of lightning".

The following night Jung had another dream of the young woman. In it he went to give her an umbrella because it was raining, but ended by handing it to her on his knees, as if she were a goddess. He told her the dream the next day, and within a week, the neurosis had vanished. The dream had told him that the woman was not the superficial little girl she seemed to be, but "had the makings of a saint". Jung explains:

I had to awaken mythological and religious ideas in her, for she belonged to that class of human beings of whom spiritual activity is demanded . . . in this case I applied no 'method', but had sensed the presence of the *numen*. My explaining this to her had accomplished the cure. Method did not matter here: what mattered was 'the fear of God.' (16)

Luckily, Jung's intuition about the woman appears to have been correct. One can imagine the damage that could be done by a doctor who subjected his patients to every "hunch" he had about them! But Jung was very careful with the resistances his patients showed. If they presented recurring resistance to the course of the analysis, then he recognised that for them the cure might be more painful than the neurosis. And this is a fact which should be taken to heart in the use of dreams for therapeutic purposes. To be healed, a person has to want to heal herself. If she does not want to, then there is nothing the therapist or dream-worker can do.

More of Jung in later chapters. He and Freud were both giants and their influence is felt everywhere in the field of dreams, with each practitioner taking what he or she wants from their work and leaving the rest. Psychoanalyst Karen Horney brought to the Freudian method a warmth and personal intensity which remove the reductive tendency within it and turn it into an heroic struggle for growth. While Freud was a pessimist, she was an optimist, even in the face of the human misery she encountered daily in her work.

She believed that in dreams "we are closer to the reality of ourselves", and the dreamer can glimpse "a world operating within him which is peculiarly his own and is more true to his feelings than the world of his illusions". She claimed that "the therapeutic value of the disillusioning process lies in the possibility that, with the weakening of the obstructive forces, the constructive forces of the real self have a chance to grow". (17)

This is interesting: we often talk about "dreams and illusions" as if they were more or less the same thing, but here Karen Horney talks about work on dreams as part of a *dis*illusioning process. She believed that dreams could be used to bring the person into contact with *reality*. This is another key concept in the proper use of dreams to heal: dream-work does not provide an escape but a confrontation, sometimes with feelings of great loss, or sadness or anger. Horney tells the story of a cynical woman who had wasted much of her life in drifting, but who had recently started to work on herself:

She dreamed that a woman who stood for everything that was fine and likeable, about to enter a religious order, was accused of some offence against it. She was condemned and exposed to public disgrace in a parade. Although the dreamer was convinced of her essential innocence, she too was participating in the parade. On the other hand, she tried to plead in her favour with a priest. The priest, though sympathetic, could do nothing for the accused. Later the accused was on a farm, not only utterly destitute but dull and half-witted. The dreamer, still in her dream, felt a heart-rending pity for the victim and wept for hours after waking. Barring details, the dreamer here says to herself: there is something fine and likeable in me; through my self-condemnation and self-destructiveness I may actually ruin my personality; my steps against such drives are ineffectual; though I want to save myself, I also avoid a real fight and, in some way, collaborate with my destructive drives. (18)

The woman's dream enacts a drama, in which the dreamer plays all the parts. The truth about her situation is revealed. But the actual work of integration and self-realisation lies before her. The dream cannot heal – only the dreamer, by choice, can set that process in motion.

Which raises an issue: if you do not know who you really are, and what is going on in your unconscious, then there is no pressure on you to change, to explore, to become your "real self". But if you begin to *know*, through dreams or other methods, you soon become conscious that you have a *choice*: to retreat from your new knowledge and live a deliberately limited life, or to embrace it and take on all the pains and pleasures of expansion and development. Choice. To pay attention to dreams means to wish to become more than an average, conditioned being, to accept that *you* are the author and director of your nightly dramas, and if you don't decide what happens next, the actors will improvise their own scenario, and steal your energy to run it!

Frances G. Wickes was a Jungian psychotherapist much preoccupied with the problem of choice. In her book *The Inner World of Choice* she uses dreams to chart the progress of individuals as they struggle up out of the darkness of neurosis. She pays particular attention to the relationship between masculine and feminine in the psyche. Jung called the image of the masculine which a woman carries within her the "animus", and the corresponding feminine image within a man, the "anima". Images of the "animus" and "anima" are common in dreams: a woman might dream of a dark, sardonic figure who will not deign to help her when she is in need (indicating a poor relationship with her "animus"); while a man might see his "anima" as a grave, mature woman who leads him to a forgotten garden (in which case his attitude towards the feminine within himself is positive). If our internal image of the opposite sex is distorted (for example, if we *really* think all women are stupid or all men cruel) it means that we cannot use and integrate the part of ourselves which identifies with the opposite sex. This is a crippling disadvantage, as you'll know if you've observed men who never cuddle their children or women who can't argue logically. Frances Wickes quotes a woman's dream:

It is early morning. Below my window are rows of young fruit trees that were set out yesterday under my direction. The gardener said this was not the place for them. The soil and drainage were wrong. I told him it was my wish they should be there and he was to follow my orders. I had a sense of satisfaction on seeing them and go down to revel in what I have done, but as I pass through, all the trees wither and die. I look back upon a dead and sterile orchard. (19)

The woman thinks of herself as all-powerful, and shuns the animus-figure gardener who tries to guide her. Her satisfaction is not in the growth of the plants, but in the domination of nature and of the gardener. If she had been prepared to accept the message of her dream, which was that nothing would grow in her garden while she rejected the gardener, she might have found ways to use her power creatively. As it was, Frances Wickes tells us that she did not accept this reading of the dream, left psychoanalysis, and returned to her bad old ways.

In this chapter we have looked at three ways of building a bridge between the conscious and the unconscious mind in order to get at the healing power of dreams; by incubation, by shamanic magic and by psychoanalysis. In the next chapter we will consider what is going on now and investigate some practical techniques for using dreams to heal.

Chapter 3

Healing with Dreams: The Pioneers

To get to the meaning of dreams, actualise dreams rather than interpret them. (Strephon Kaplan Williams in *The Dreamwork Manual*) (20)

The psychoanalysts we were looking at in the previous chapter were all in the business of *interpreting* dreams, that is to say, translating the symbolic code of the dream into a form which the dreamer could understand, with a meaning which he could absorb. This means that, on the whole, the dream's message is being taken in *via the intellect*, though of course it may well go on to affect the emotions and the body. But basically interpretation is an intellectual technique and there are many dream-workers who do not like that and feel there are better ways to get to the matter of a dream, by "actualising" rather than interpreting.

In order to avoid being too intellectual, let us look straight away at three examples of "actualisation" of dreams. The first is from psychotherapist Arnold Mindell. In his book *Working with the dreaming body* he tells the story of a man dying of stomach cancer who dreamt that he had an incurable disease and that the medicine for it was "like a bomb". Mindell, who knew nothing of this dream, visited the man in hospital while he was in great pain. Following a hunch, Mindell asked him not to try to minimise the pain but instead to *amplify* it. The man did so: "he pushed his stomach out and kept pushing and pressing and exaggerating the pain until he felt he were going to explode." Finally he cried out "Oh Arny, I just want to explode!" Mindell reports that, after this session, the man began to feel better and was allowed home from hospital – in fact he lived for another few years. Mindell believes that what cured him was the body being able to act out what the psyche knew already: that this quiet, repressed man needed to *express* himself. The pressure to do so had built up unregarded for so long that the impulse to *express* had become the impulse to *explode*. (21)

In our second example a young woman (a friend of mine who is an enthusiastic dream-worker) dreamed that she was standing on the bank of a wide, fast-flowing river. She was frightened of slipping in and being swept away by the water, but also awed and thrilled by the power of the current. The next day she was jogging along the banks of the muddy little apology-for-a-river which flowed through her local park. Actually it had been raining and the river was in spate and looked quite impressive. She was reminded of the river of her dream.

Later, when she was feeling exhausted and ready to give up, she thought of the effortless power of the river of her dream, and she imagined it flowing through her body. Her limbs lightened, her lungs expanded, the strain was lifted from her. The air, like the water of a great river, supported her and carried her along.

The third story is from a dream workshop I was running for women, when I had split everybody into groups, and people were acting out the different elements of their dreams. When I went to watch the group which contained my friend Nora, I was amazed: Nora was such a thoroughly *nice* person, who refused to row with her husband however unpleasant he might be, and never raised her voice to her children. But here she was, eyes flashing, body throbbing out energy, voice rich and croaky, acting out the "wicked witch" from a childhood dream. She was magnificent and terrifying. "If only she would allow some of that power out into her life," I thought, "then her grumpy husband would have something to look out for!"

What these three dreamers have in common is that they did not unpick and interpret their dreams; instead they became active and *took* something from the dream into their waking behaviour. They roused themselves from the passivity which traps most of us for most of our lives (quite unnecessarily of course!) They "actualised" something latent within them which had so far only shown itself in dream.

And this is just what the Senoi people, who live in the central highlands of Malaysia, teach their children to do, according to anthropologist Kilton Stewart. The Senoi, he claimed, are remarkable in that there is no violent crime, armed conflict or mental illness within their boundaries. All because the dream-work which they practise produces such a high level of psychological integration. So what is this wonderful dream-work? (I will optimistically use the present tense for describing the Senoi, hoping that they have not lost this tradition since Stewart visited them in 1935.)

For a start, both adults and children are encouraged to pay great attention to their dreams, and to endeavour to bring conscious control into the dream-world. Thus, if a Senoi boy dreams he meets a hostile animal or person, he is instructed to call on his "dream-helpers" to aid him to kill or subdue the adversary, so that its spirit will become an ally and help him in the future.

If he dreams he is falling, he should not panic but relax and enjoy himself because "falling is the quickest way to get in contact with the spirit world". Later in life, if he dreams of sexual intercourse, even if it is with someone tabooed in the waking world, he is to continue the dream to orgasm, and then ask the dream-lover for a song to take back. In general, pleasant dreams are continued until the dreamer finds something of beauty which can be brought back for the tribe.

All these techniques depend upon two things: firstly, on an understanding of the *difference* between the waking world and the dream-world, and a clear awareness of which world you are in at the time; and secondly, on an acceptance of the idea that power won in one world can be used in the other, and, what is more, that what appears to be negative in one world can be turned into something positive in the other. So, for example, if you *dream* of behaving cruelly to someone, in *waking* life you can go out of your way to be kind to him; or, if a boy dreams of harming another boy, the *other* boy may be instructed by his parents to bring the dreamer a present, to nullify the latent hostility between the two of them. (22)

Before we move on I must mention that the Senoi are such paragons that some people recently have begun to doubt whether they really exist. All I can say is that if they don't, they ought to, and I congratulate Kilton Stewart on the invention of a most useful and suggestive modern myth! For the story of the Senoi has been very influential in changing our thinking about dreaming in what I feel is a healthy way: previously dream-work concentrated on the negative – you had your dreams analysed in order to see what was *wrong* with you. But, now, dream-work techniques are becoming popular which put most of the stress on the *positive*, demanding that the dreamer actively participate in exploring and expanding his personal world. The two most popular techniques (under which headings most other techniques can be grouped) are Active Imagination and Gestalt. Let us look at each in turn.

Jungian Marie Louise von Franz defines Active Imagination thus:

Active Imagination is a certain way of meditating imaginatively by which one may deliberately enter into contact with the unconscious and make a conscious connection with psychic phenomena. (23)

This technique takes the faculty of image-making which is

effortlessly at work in dreams and develops it so that it can be used while you are awake. This is quite tricky to do because the ego is always trying to intervene and censor the material which emerges by labelling it "absurd", "boring", "obscene" and so on. There is also the ever-present tendency to fall asleep!

The very simplest sort of Active Imagination would be to lie in bed in the morning, run over a dream from the night before, and then continue it or change it while awake yet relaxed and not too far away from the dream state. In this mood it is possible to experiment and play around with various different outcomes of a dream. But it is not as easy as it sounds – I still can't bring myself to get into any of those dirty swimming-pools!

One of the most infuriating things about dreaming is that most dreams are unresolved, that is, the story they tell does not "end" satisfactorily. Also, many dreams, although fascinating and glistening with apparent meaning, are garbled, contradictory and difficult to grasp. It is tempting in such cases to feel that the game is not worth the candle and give up trying to make sense of the nonsense. But particularly when we have a series of dreams which seem to be related, or one theme keeps recurring, we feel the need to get to the bottom of things and find out what is going on – this especially if our waking life is not going well.

Strephon Kaplan Williams is an inventive American psychotherapist who specialises in dream-work. If you can understand his Californian personal-growth-world jargon, you will find that he has some very good ideas for harnessing the healing power of dreams. He takes as his inspiration both Jung and the Senoi, and most of his techniques are based on Active Imagination. Let us see how he develops the idea of "dream re-entry" which we have already looked at in its simplest form:

Essentially this means re-entering or re-doing the dream in some form with the intention of bringing resolution to certain situations and elements in the dream. This re-entry or revision is done in the waking state usually by entering into a semi-trance condition, re-experiencing the dream, putting the intention for seeking resolution into it, and letting go and seeing how the imagery and dialogue develop. (24)

Here is an example which Williams gives in his book: a woman dreams that some seals are being transported in a truck and that two small ones are frozen, to be thawed out later. But it turns out that one of these is dead and the other dying. A woman suggests to the dreamer that she take them out and see what the situation really is, but the dreamer doesn't want to make things worse and decides to leave the seals alone.

In her first dream re-entry session, the woman talks to the seals and asks them who they are. They tell her they are her "hurt feelings" and claim that she has ignored them to the point that they are very ill. Then she re-lives the dream, this time taking the seals' explanations into account, getting them out of the van, cleaning and massaging them, caring for them, bringing the dead one back to life. Finally she moves them into a swimming-pool, and then into the sea where they can care for themselves, but where she can visit them once in a while. She ends by asking the seals how they would like her to handle her feelings differently and they tell her:

Watch them, and when they are hurt in any way, stand up for them, protect them. Don't give to everybody else at their (our) expense and don't let other people injure them (us). (25)

The woman changed the outcome of her dream. Whether this inner change effected an outer one we do not know, but the example clearly shows the principle upon which this sort of dream-work is founded: the idea that if you can organize your inner world by re-balancing the different elements operating within your psyche in a more positive way, then you may see a similar re-balancing happening in your relationship with the outer world.

The effect of working with dreams is subtle, usually

gradual: people change and heal themselves in their own time and in their own way. It is very important to understand that the relationship which you build up between your waking and your dreaming mind is a delicate, tenuous affair and *must remain so*. If the unconscious is bullied or dominated it will simply withdraw its cooperation and find other ways of making itself felt, which may be extremely awkward or painful. Therefore there is no way of "proving" to people who have not done it that dream-work works or that dream-work can heal. You just have to say to them that "the proof of the pudding is in the eating", and you cannot eat someone else's pudding for them any more than you can dream someone else's dreams!

That said, I must admit that the Gestalt technique when applied to dreams does sometimes have stunning results. It is a method borrowed from the Gestalt school of psychotherapy founded by Fritz Perls, and it is based on the principle that all the elements of a dream are parts of the dreamer, split off from his ego and struggling to come into relation with each other. In order to integrate all these parts the dreamer must "become" each one in turn and experience the dream from his, her or its point of view. Once the different identities are established they can talk or fight with each other (or communicate in some other way) until a resolution is achieved. No judgements, criticisms or interpretations are allowed, but the dreamer is encouraged to act out physically what he is experiencing by, for instance, changing positions or changing voice. Gestalt has to be done, at least initially, under the supervision of someone expert in the technique, because sometimes people are surprised and taken aback by the emotions they experience in the different roles. And like all active dream-work methods it should only be done by individuals with a stable psychological foundation.

The procedure is for the dreamer to relax, let the breath settle, and shut his eyes. Then he tells the dream in the present tense, starting with the word "I". This is to make the dream immediate and real and to prevent the censoring mind from creeping in to change things. The leader will then ask the dreamer to tell the dream from the point of view of another element or character in the dream. It's at this stage that the dreamer may amaze himself with the ease with which he "becomes" a witch or even a garage, or he may find it very difficult and have to be eased and encouraged into letting go. (I would like to make it clear that the person is not in some kind of deep hypnotic trance while he is doing the work – his attention is focused on the dream but he should be perfectly aware of what is going on around him in the room.)

The leader may ask the dreamer to become several more elements from his dream, putting questions such as "how do you feel?", asking for clarification, and occasionally, if it feels right, making suggestions ("Are you angry about the mess the dog has made?") But he must not bully the dreamer into experiencing anything which is not his.

The dreamer can then begin to dialogue with any of the other identities in the dream, playing the part of himself *and* the other element. Sometimes it will be appropriate to explore some part of the dream in depth. Sometimes the dreamer will react quite spontaneously to something he has said while in a role and suddenly "see" what the dream is all about. He may laugh, or more rarely, cry. In some cases it does not take long to reach a resolution point; in others it is a long, laborious business; in yet others nothing significant comes up, in which case there's either very strong resistance or the dream is not a rich one. Anyway, it is better to give up than push the dreamer, unless you are sure you know what you are doing.

You *can* do Gestalt work on your own, either by acting it out loud, if you are that kind of person, or by writing it down very quickly as it happens, trying not to censor or be critical of what is coming into your head. You can also "do

43

it in your head", but, take my advice, don't do it while you are driving because you can get carried away and find that you are sailing down the outside lane at ninety miles an hour! It is quite tricky to do it on your own because there is a temptation to drift into daydream or give up if things are less than fascinating straightaway. And it is important to remember that *you* are in control, and the object of the exercise is not to harrow or punish yourself. Nightmares are best not worked on alone until you have acquired some expertise in the technique.

Here is an example of a piece of written Gestalt work from a member of the dream-group. The dreamer is a woman involved at the time of the dream in a problematical relationship with a charming, rather introverted man.

I am in a concentration camp. We are all about to die. Then, for no apparent reason, my male companion and myself are told we can go free. I am immensely relieved, but my companion says he cannot bear the thought of freedom and asks to die with the rest. Amused, the sadistic commandant looks on. I am frozen with horror and don't know what to say. If I show understanding for my companion I may be sent off to die with him. If I say I disagree and try to persuade him to leave, he will think I am betraying him.

The dreamer did not have a clue what the dream was about, so first she "became" the companion and wrote down his feelings:

COMPANION: I just can't stand any more of this. I would sooner die with the others than live on just to be prey to hurt again. I can't stand any more uncertainty and pain. You can't trust them anyway. Better to be dead. Quickly.

DREAMER: But why do you think you were chosen for freedom?

COMPANION: Just a whim. No rhyme or reason. Kill you as soon as look at you. I'm no more deserving to live than the rest of them. I'm autistic with fear.

The dreamer then "became" the commandant:

DREAMER: Why did you choose these two for freedom?

COMMANDANT: The rest are no use. These two have will, stronger than mine. I cannot kill them. They can only kill themselves. It's a trick. I fooled one but not the other. He wants to die. Good. A victory for us.

DREAMER: Who are you?

COMMANDANT: The forces of darkness and ignorance of course. The mockers.

DREAMER: Why are they [the dreamer and her companion] so afraid of you?

COMMANDANT: I don't know. Since it's only a trick. We are only a mask for the testers. They don't realise that. If they did, the game would be up.

DREAMER: How could they recognise that? What could they do?

COMMANDANT: She has the right idea. But she mustn't be infected by his terror.

DREAMER: He needs to go through the gate, doesn't he?

COMMANDANT: He has been. But he looked back and froze. He has to be unfrozen.

This work is of course not untouched by the dreamer's personal associations (for instance, "going through the gate" meant for her "committing yourself"), but it is still possible to see how the technique unpacked the dream in a way that surprised the dreamer and gave her information which was very relevant for her situation. I do not want to interpret the dream because that is against the spirit of Gestalt, but I can say that the dreamer was disturbed to recognise that the companion (her lover in thin disguise) had such a negative outlook in regard both to the idea of freedom and to commitment to herself. It seemed that in order to "save herself" she would have to leave him behind. Unless she could unfreeze him   She tried to do that, but failed, and a few weeks later they parted. When she bumped into him a year later her life had moved into a new and stimulating phase while he was unemployed and depressed. She was sad to see this but recognised that she could not have saved him: it was his own choice to take the negative path.

Chris Murray is a social-worker and counsellor who uses Gestalt both in his day-job dealing with mentally-ill people and in evening sessions with private clients. He says that people quite often come to him with a dream saying "I know it's important, but I don't know what it means." Chris will first ask them what their current problems are – trouble with a partner, disturbance at work, a difficult decision of some sort – and then work with the dream to find out what is causing the trouble. Sometimes people only need one session to unlock the dream and see what needs to be done. Others (for instance those who are under psychiatric care and have perhaps suffered trauma in childhood) may require many sessions.

One of Chris's rules, while doing Gestalt work, is not to let people get away with saying "*it* hurts" when what they really mean is "*I* hurt". If he feels someone will need pushing to face up to what is wrong he will make a "contract" with them, whereby he tells them the kinds of thing he will need to do (such as take on the role of a bullying parent) and promises to stay with the work until the end, as long as the client promises to stick with it too. After using Gestalt to open up the psychological picture, Chris may switch to techniques from Transactional Analysis. This might involve acting out dialogues between, say, the "scared child" and the "bullying parent", figures suggested by the content of the dream in question.

A woman was in hospital with a recurring back problem and was being examined with a view to yet another operation on her back. In a rather sneering, sexist way the consultant remarked that it was probably really a sexual problem. At this point Chris had a dream-work session with the woman and she told him of a dream which bothered her where she was standing outside her own house watching it burn down. She wondered why she was outside while all her family were inside burning to death, and felt that the whole thing was somehow her fault. During the course of the dream-work she revealed that she had been sexually abused as a child, and started to talk about it for the first time in detail. Gradually her feelings of rage and guilt were released and her back pain began to ease too. It would seem that the dream was the key to the healing process.

Gestalt is a very useful method for tackling psychological problems; it aims, literally, to *heal*, that is, to "make a whole" out of fragmented, warring parts of the psyche. But when it comes to the healing of *physical* complaints, it is a more difficult tool to use, except in the hands of a trained therapist. Nonetheless, there *is* a relationship between dreams and the body, for certainly there are many cases when a dream contains a message for the waking mind about the condition of the body. The following dream illustrates this clearly and was told to me, at the time, by the young man concerned. I was closely involved in the subsequent development of his situation and so I can vouch for the accuracy of this report.

The young man was in hospital with a mysterious, as yet undiagnosed illness. One night he had an extraordinarily vivid dream: he dreamed that his girlfriend came in to visit him and announced that she had met another man at a party and was going to leave him and go off with this new man. Then he found himself cut off from all his friends, and was puzzled and hurt by the situation. Worst of all, he was forced to marry a certain woman whom, in waking life, he heartily disliked – she was a widow whose husband had died of cancer. The dream thoroughly upset him, and felt so real that it took his girlfriend quite some time to convince him that she loved him and had no intention of leaving him for another man.

Sadly, the dream's meaning soon became clear, when the man's illness was diagnosed: he had a serious form of cancer and very little chance of surviving it. His dream had told him of the gravity of his condition in three ways: firstly, his girlfriend would replace him, which of course she did eventually, long after his death; secondly, he would be cut off from his friends – by death; and thirdly, he would be "married" against his will to a death-bringer. Although the young man did not talk much about his dream, it doubtless began to prepare him psychologically for what was to happen to him. It did not "heal" him in the sense of making him well, but it did tell the "whole" if bitter truth about his condition.

Arnold Mindell has written several books exploring the relationship between the unconscious mind and the body. He talks about an entity he calls the "dreambody", which is a subtle body, seemingly created out of psychic energy. He explains:

Today, in the 'civilised' world, the body is composed of heart, lungs, RNA, bacteria, cells and diseases. In contrast, the dreambody is created by individual experience, personal descriptions of signals, sensations and fantasies which do not necessarily conform to collective materialistic definitions. (26)

That is as near as Mindell gets to a definition, but we must not blame him for his vagueness – he is trying to convey something very difficult, something not normally talked about because it is so nebulous and elusive, which belongs to the deep-sea realm of unconsciousness, and therefore appears distorted when lifted out of its element into the clear air of daytime consciousness. So how does this "dreambody" relate to dreams?

In dreambody work dreams appear as pictorialisations of body processes that are happening *now*. One experiences how the body is pressured by the dream world and how dreams are intimately connected to body problems. (27)

Mindell tells how a little girl with a tumour on her back was brought to see him. She was thought to be very near to death, and her doctors told him that she was an unhappy child. She told him that she had dreamed of letting go of the safety fences round a very dangerous lake. Then, encouraged by Mindell to play, she lay down on the floor and said she wanted to fly. With some trepidation he took off the corset she wore to protect her back and played at flying with her. The little girl informed him that she was "going away to another world, a beautiful world where there are strange planets". But then she cried and said she did not want to leave Arny because she liked flying with him. "I'll come down for a while to be with you," she said. Mindell continues:

The little girl improved rapidly and soon she could take off her corset, and even the tumour disappeared. It was obviously her process to come back down to the earth for a while. More specifically it was her process to 'fly'. That is, to play kinaesthetically and be free to move about. Her process started out in a kinaesthetic channel and moved into a visual one, when she was seeing the planets and clouds. Then she ended in a proprioceptive channel, feeling the sadness of leaving this earth. (28)

This might sound rather like a miracle cure, but, to be fair to Mindell, he also gives examples of people *not* cured by dreambody work, saying that it was their "process" to die. Again, if you can accept the American psycho-jargon, he has some very intriguing ideas which sound far-fetched at first but begin to grow on you with perseverance.

For instance, I woke up the other morning with very restless legs. Although I was tired and had not slept well my legs insisted I got up and went for a long walk. While we were walking they "told" me that they were very angry that I tried to cut off the energy coming through them, and they would continue to cause me trouble like this if I did not listen to them. In fact, daft though it may sound, "listening to my legs" opened the floodgates and there followed a day of emotional release: I cried, I expressed my anger and frustration, I poured out all my resentments against the people who I thought were making heavy demands on me. And, as you know, my reluctance to "plunge" into the world of emotion is one of the things my dreams are always nagging me about. Now my legs are nagging too. It seems there will be no escape!

In the dream-group it was interesting to notice how people changed physically while acting out different roles from their dreams: if Jane was "being" a garage, then she would plonk herself down on her hands and knees and stay rigid and immobile, as if she really were a building and not a person! If Sarah was "being" a little girl, her face would soften and relax into the face of an eight-year-old. And many places which crop up commonly in dreams (house, cave, attic, garden) have obvious correspondances in the body (whole body, womb, brain, organs connected with fertility). When symbols like these occur, it is worth trying out the simple physical interpretation first: if you dream of being in a leaky, unsound attic with rotting floor boards, how are you using your brain at the moment? Are you avoiding real thought? Are you wasting mental energy in repetitive daydreams?

But apart from delightful sensations of flying, sexual bliss and other sorts of exhilaration, dreaming brings us some very painful experiences. I for one have been more harrowed and terrified in my dream-life than in my waking life. So if we are talking about healing via dreams, we must consider what can be done about nightmares. (I would not include anxiety dreams in this category, unless they are frightening enough to wake you up, and leave a residue of terror in the mind.)

It is usually stated in dream-books that there are two sorts of nightmare: the night *terror*, from which the dreamer wakes with a shriek and a pounding heart but with little memory of what caused the terror; and the nightmare proper which is a dream with very distressing or disturbing content from which the dreamer may or may not awake suddenly.

The night-terror, or "incubus attack", usually occurs during one of the first two periods of non-dreaming sleep, and is accompanied by a sense of falling, being crushed or otherwise hastened to destruction. One theory is that it is caused by some disturbance of the waking-up process, but nobody really knows for sure. Dream-books will usually tell you that there is no point in trying to find out what "message" a night-terror is passing on, because it has little or no content and does not come from the usual dreaming level of the mind. But if you, like me, have had these attacks regularly from childhood, you may want to think a little more about them. I have noticed that I tend to have these attacks when I have been stretching my mind, doing a lot of thinking and conceptualising. I have also noticed that, when I have been able to remember an image on waking up, it has usually had to do with something breaking through into the room (the walls are caving in), or myself being crushed (by something *immensely* heavy), or threatened (by entities so vast and abstract as to be almost inconceivable). In other words, these images have been on a scale or of a nature so removed from my ordinary preoccupations as to give me a sense of being invaded or annihilated by something extremely powerful and alien. I'm not about to claim that I have been visited by creatures from another space-time continuum (though maybe that's what they are!), but I am suggesting that night-terrors may actually be a sudden perception on the part of the dreamer of concepts from the world of abstraction and pure thought. Unless you are a mathematician, such concepts will certainly appear as alien and threatening, because they are so awesome and unfamiliar. If this is true (and of course it may just apply to me, not to others who suffer from these attacks), then you might expect to have them in periods of growth and expansion of consciousness. As far as I am concerned this seems to be the case and I no longer feel miserable when I go through a spell of having night-terrors: something vast, powerful and potentially creative *is* breaking through momentarily into my mind – OK, fine – I've always wanted to make my world bigger and perhaps these experiences can help me do that!

In fact, night-terrors are rare; the vast majority of bad dreams are nightmares, much easier to work with because we can usually recall some if not all of the content. Ann

Faraday, author of *Dreampower* and *The Dream Game* writes:

My own work on dreams indicates that a recurring nightmare invariably indicates a deep split within the personality, and the more severe the nightmare the more severe the split. My experience has been, however, that intensive work with nightmares . . . results not only in their disappearance but also in the healing of the split, with the release of an enormous amount of energy for constructive living. (29)

Ann Faraday has found another idea from Gestalt useful in working on nightmares – the notion of "topdogs" and "underdogs": "topdog" being the bullying, bossy figure who wants everything done *his* way, "underdog" the expression of some basic need which has been suppressed or ignored. She explains:

A 'self-punishment' nightmare occurs whenever underdog has defied topdog during the day, in which case topdog hounds him at night in order to regain control over him. On the other hand whenever topdog has denied underdog a really basic need during the day, underdog, driven to the end of his tether, comes out in a thoroughly nasty way at night. In either case it is a fight to the death, which accounts for the feeling of dread and terror in the nightmare itself. (30)

"Topdog" might appear in a nightmare as a threatening, bullying figure who mocks your attempts to escape from a burning building; while "underdog" might well represent himself as the wilful, uncontrollable toddler who runs away from you down endless corridors, whom you can never quite catch, although you know you must.

Ann Faraday points out that it is important to know whether your nightmare adversary is "topdog" or "underdog", because while "underdog" can and should be integrated into the personality, "topdog" cannot be incorporated since he would want to dominate and rule the roost completely; he must therefore be listened to but stripped of his absolute power and turned from a master into a servant. With this in mind, various techniques (see next chapter for details) of Active Imagination and Gestalt can be tried with nightmares. It is interesting to see that in the example of Gestalt which I quoted earlier, the evil, sadistic commandant dissolves, under Gestalt interrogation, into an intriguing and much less frightening figure, and ends up almost as an ally. This is not surprising, of course, because we make our own monsters and obviously we can take back the clay we made them with and form it into something more congenial, if we so wish.

If the "topdog"/"underdog" theory does not help sort out what is happening in a nightmare, then you might be facing what the Jungians call the "shadow". The "shadow" is that part of the unconscious personality which is made up of qualities which we reject or repress in ourselves, but which, nevertheless, belong to us. If we think of ourselves as nice and good, the shadow who crops up in our dreams will be selfish and wicked. But if we are wicked and hard in our waking lives, the shadow may appear as a noble and kindly figure. It will usually be represented by a person of the same sex as the dreamer, which helps distinguish it from "animus" and "anima" figures. Marie Louise von Franz remarks that "the shadow usually contains values that are needed by consciousness, but that exist in a form that makes it difficult to integrate them into one's life". The qualities of the shadow may not, in themselves, be either good or bad, but they are present in the psyche and need to be recognised and assimilated or they may turn destructive. Von Franz continues:

Divining in advance whether our dark partner symbolises a short-coming that we should overcome or a meaningful bit of life that we should accept – this is one of the most difficult problems that we encounter on the way to individuation. (31)

In his autobiography Jung describes many dream-encounters with the shadow. Once, while in Tunis, he dreamed of wrestling with a handsome young Arab prince who tries to kill him by drowning, but whom he finally manages to subdue. Jung recognises the dusky man as the shadow, as

that part of my personality which had become invisible under the influence and the pressure of being European . . . this part stands in unconscious opposition to myself, and indeed, I attempt to suppress it. In keeping with its nature, it wishes to make me unconscious (force me under water) so as to kill me; but my aim is, through insight, to make it more conscious, so that we can find a common modus vivendi. (32)

Whether nightmares represent struggles between "top-dog" and "underdog", confrontations with the shadow, or simply a grave situation happening in our waking lives, they are always about *conflict*. The conflict can be futile, destructive, or creative, depending on our attitude towards it. There is tremendous energy locked up in the hideous images of nightmares: if we are willing to follow the example of Beauty when she meets the Beast and take time to penetrate beneath appearances, we may be able to win back some of that energy for ourselves.

Chapter 4

Stepping into the Unknown

Dream-work as self-development

The breeze at dawn has secrets to tell you
                    Don't go back to sleep.
You must ask for what you really want.
                    Don't go back to sleep.
People are going back and forth across the doorsill
                    where the two worlds touch.
The door is round and open.
                    Don't go back to sleep.
(Jelaluddin Rumi) (33)

One of the big questions which most of us shy away from asking in the course of our lives is: "What do I *really* want?" It sounds like a simple question, but it is actually very difficult to answer — try it and see! You'll find that you easily discover all sorts of little "wants": to find a satisfying job, to fall in love, to have a baby, earn more money, and so on. But then you will need to look beyond all these entirely natural wishes and ask "What are my *long-term* goals? What am I *really* aiming for?"

If we are working with dreams it is particularly important for us to be clear about what we are aiming for, because what we search for in this realm will surely condition what we find. While we are talking about the therapeutic aspect of dream-work there is little problem, because we are simply aiming for ease from pain, whether it be physical or psychological, and to be "just normal" seems a very desirable thing. But if we have healed our wounds and achieved some kind of wholeness and balance, what then? Is "normality" what we *really* want? If it truly is (and of course it is, for perhaps the vast majority of people) then there is not much point in continuing to work with dreams. Because at the next stage of dream-work we confront a barrier which, if crossed, leaves the "normal" world behind.

We are now at a stage where, in order to extract more from dreams, we have to change our attitude towards them: we have to learn to be active and passive at the same time, to be cunning and ingenious, and, above all, persistent in exploring this unfamiliar world. But also we must be open-minded: we are stepping into the unknown and can have no idea of what will happen to us there. If we do have some sort of idea, then it is not the "unknown" we are entering! In fact, what we must do is attempt to come to terms with the unconscious. We cannot do that on our own terms. On the other hand, we certainly should not do it entirely on the terms imposed by the unconscious – that way leads to delusion at the least and psychotic breakdown at the worst.

How do we make a relationship between the conscious and the unconscious which protects the integrity of both but allows change and transformation to occur? Jung thought long and hard about this problem and came up with the idea that the bridge between the two realms was the "transcendent function":

the tendency of the conscious and the unconscious are the two factors that together make up the transcendent function. It is called 'transcendent' because it makes the transition from one attitude to another organically possible, without loss of the unconscious. (34)

As far as I understand it, the "transcendent function" is simply the sort of mental activity which builds that bridge. But if this seems a slippery idea to you at first, don't worry: you will see it in action in the rest of this chapter. I cannot pretend that it is an easy thing to investigate the contents of the unconscious: it requires a leap of faith and imagination just to kick the "transcendent function" into action.

Jung said that the first thing you needed, in order to produce the "transcendent function", was a source of "unconscious material". Either dreams or waking fantasy can be used to provide this material, which is then worked on using the various techniques of Active Imagination. Jung noted that people would either naturally tend towards a non-intellectual "creative formulation" of the material (they would tend to make a picture or a story of it), *or* they would tend immediately to attempt to "understand" it intellectually. But he thought both tendencies were essential and should, ideally, be alternated while the work was going on. (This is in fact a good guideline for all dream-work – vary your approach to dreams and don't avoid the techniques you find most difficult, for they may well be the most useful for you.)

During the production and formulation of the material, Jung said, the unconscious must take the lead, but once this is done, it was vital for the ego to take over, because conscious and unconscious minds are equal in this game and each must be allowed to have its say. An excellent method of achieving this is to have a *dialogue* between what Jung calls the "other voice" (the voice of the dream or fantasy) and the normal waking ego. For example, if you drew a picture of a decrepit old man from a dream, your dialogue would be between him (coming through you, of course) and you. Jung wrote of the crucial importance of developing this ability to dialogue, to "let the other man's argument count". He said that:

to the degree that [a person] does not admit the validity of the other person, he denies the "other" within himself the right to exist – and vice versa. The capacity for inner dialogue is a touchstone for outer objectivity. (35)

It is easy to see how the ability to dialogue like this develops flexibility and openness, stimulates the imagination via conflict, and *challenges* the ego without threatening the necessary foundations upon which a person has built his life. Foundations *can* be threatened and changed, but only after a great deal of preliminary work has been done. Jung continued:

the shuttling to and fro of arguments and affects represents the transcendent function of opposites. The confrontation of the two positions generates a tension charged with energy and creates a living, third thing . . . a living birth which leads to a new level of being, a new situation. The transcendent function manifests itself as a quality of conjoined opposites. So long as these are kept apart – naturally for the purpose of avoiding conflict – they do not function and remain inert. (36)

The ability to endure and observe conflict within oneself without a premature "taking sides" is a prerequisite for dream-work once past the "isn't it fascinating?" stage. It is also, as Jung pointed out, a practice which helps a person break his dependence on his analyst or group-leader so that he can "attain liberation by his own efforts and find the courage to be himself".

Jung's work on dreams is like an underground river, rich in valuable minerals, which feeds the roots of our contemporary dream-work; but, before we move on to look at that, I would like to introduce you to someone outside the mainstream, who has a different but equally constructive view of dreams. His name is Seth and he is a "discarnate entity" who communicates with us via an American medium called Jane Roberts. Don't be put off by the introduction – Seth is a charming, humorous and disconcertingly intelligent entity, and indeed Jane Roberts is an intelligent, well-balanced woman, creative in her own right. Seth "comes through" while Jane is in a light trance and her husband, Robert, takes notes of what he says. Seth's suggestions on how dreams can be used to expand the range of consciousness are particularly relevant to us: he presumes that curiosity about the nature of the universe and of consciousness is the motivating force for dream-work rather than merely the drive to solve personal problems. He says:

The true art of dreaming is a *science* long forgotten by your world. Such an art, pursued, trains the mind in a new kind of consciousness – one that is equally at home in either existence, well-grounded and secure in each. Almost anyone can become a satisfied and productive *amateur* in this art-science; but its true fulfilment takes years of training, a strong sense of purpose, and a dedication – as does any true vocation.

To some extent, a natural talent is a prerequisite for such a true dream-art scientist. A sense of daring, exploration, independence, and spontaneity is required. Such a work is a joy. There are some such people who are quite unrecognised by your societies, because the particular gifts involved are given zero priority. But the *talent* still exists. (37)

The "dream-art scientist" is of course someone who knows how to activate and use the *transcendent function*, who can study his own subjective experiences with a degree of objectivity, not in order to reduce their personal meaning, but in order to make of them a tool for digging into the unknown. As Seth says, "I am suggesting ways in which the unknown reality can become a known one."

Seth suggests multifarious techniques for exploring the world of dreams for yourself. For instance:

Look around you in the dream state. Try to expand any location in which you find yourself. If you are in a house remember to look out of the window. And once you walk to that window, a scene will appear. You can walk out of that dream house into another environment; and theoretically at least you can explore that world, and the space within it will expand. There will be no spot in the dream where the environment will cease. (38)

Seth is pushing us to discover the nature of the dream-world by means of *active investigation*, in order to understand the *different set of rules* which apply there.

We can see his methods in action when he helps Jane Roberts deal with a disturbing nightmare which she has after a few days of "depression and brooding". Jane dreamed that while "out of her body" in her own room she was attacked by "a big black thing like a bloated, blurred human form, but larger and very solid". The thing bit her, tried to drag her into a cupboard, and pressed down upon her. She knew she was dreaming but that didn't stop her feeling absolutely terrified as she tried to fight the thing off. Its intent was, she was sure, "to maul me up as much as possible, if not to kill me outright". Seth explains:

The energy behind his [he calls Jane by a man's name "Rubert" during these sessions for reasons too complex to go into here] 'black thing' was the energy of hidden fears . . . [it] was actually a rather clumsy lower-dimensional animal, a provoked dumb dog of other dimensions who then attacked him, symbolically, by biting . . . the evil that Rubert imagined he was projecting outward does not exist, but because he believed it did, he formed the materialisation from his fears. It was the shape of his recent depression. In larger terms, there is no evil, only your own lack of perception, but I know this is difficult for you to accept. (39)

Seth's clear, straightforward approach is a useful astringent when wandering in the murky depths which the purple prose of certain dream-workers tends to create. It must be borne in mind that it is easy to be infected by the atmosphere of the unconscious world so that the mental level lowers and one wallows in fascinating, suggestive vagueness which, I am afraid, leads in the end not to self-development and illumination, but to dopeyness and sleep. The clarity of a well-organised but open mind is a most essential tool when dealing with dreams and the unconscious. Dream-work should never be an excuse for sloppy thinking!

Now, it is possible for an individual to acquire a lot of insight into the meaning of her dreams by working alone – by keeping a dream diary faithfully, noticing themes, perhaps doing Active Imagination exercises and dialoguing with dream characters. But eventually, if she wants to progress, she must join a dream-group. Then she will begin to learn, not just about her own dreams, but about the process of dreaming. The group will curb the tendency we all have to turn inward and be preoccupied with our own world, by demanding that she turn outward and pay attention to other people's dreams. A group is also a safety net which will catch anyone who is using dreams to fuel delusions of grandeur! But its greatest advantage is a pooling of energy, creativity and enthusiasm, and the possibility that it may lead its members to the gates of a real way of knowledge.

You may be lucky and find that, just when you want it, there is a dream-group operating in your locality which suits your needs. However this is pretty unlikely! It is more probable that either there will not be a dream-group, or there will be one whose methods you do not like. In that case you may want to start your own, either by inviting friends and acquaintances you know to be interested in dreams to join, or by advertising for like-minded people in the paper and on local radio. (They usually have a chat-show which is always short of material and may even invite you in for an interview.)

Each dream-group is different, and will find its own way of working, but I would like to pass on a few guidelines, which may save you wasting time and falling into unnecessary traps. 1) Don't make up numbers by inviting dilettantes who will not make any real effort to record their dreams and only come out of idle curiosity! 2) Try to have a minimum of five people at each meeting. Of course dream-work can be done with two or three people, but the energy level will be noticeably higher if you have a proper "group". 3) Arrange that you have at least one person present who, by virtue of professional qualifications, general level of maturity, or experience in dream or other psychological work, is able to guide the group away from time-wasting self-indulgence and keep course for genuine exploration and investigation. He or she (or you, if it is you) will also be able to keep an eye open for the odd unstable individual who really should not be working with dreams until he has sorted himself out in other ways. 4) Make a rule of confidentiality, that is that nothing reported about dreams inside the group will be repeated outside it. People unwittingly reveal a great deal about themselves when they tell their dreams, and although *you* would not use that information against them, a person outside the group who gets hold of a juicy tit-bit might not possess the same level of integrity.

My own dream-group followed this advice, with great success. I will tell you more about how we organised ourselves and what we discovered, but please do not feel that it has to be done exactly this way. Take what you want from our techniques and ideas, but be sure to invent some of your own. (I must reassure you that I am not breaking the rule of confidentiality just mentioned when I quote from the group's experience: I called a special meeting of the group and asked their permission to use material from their dreams and our discussions. They were all happy to give it.)

I had been recording my dreams for years and reading widely on the subject, and was experimenting with using dreams as inspiration for creative writing. The friend with whom I ran the group in partnership (whose name, strangely enough, is the same as mine, except that she spells her first name "Lynne" instead of "Lyn") is a psychiatrist who is interested in dreams from both a clinical and a philosophical point of view. We hoped that our complimentary interests and talents would make a good basis for the group.

They were a mixed bag of people: a university lecturer of strong Christian faith, a teacher of difficult children who studied astrology, a lawyer, a writer, two housewives, a computer-programmer, and various others who attended for a week or two at various times and left having done some good work. A core-group of six stayed together for about two years, meeting once a week for two-hour sessions. Our avowed aim was the "active investigation of dreams and dreaming".

We decided to make it a condition of entry to the group that people should start keeping a dream diary. Not only did this demand basic commitment, but it ensured that people began trying hard to *remember* their dreams, so that we had something to work on. A dream-group cannot operate unless it has dreams to work on! So we would begin each meeting by getting a report from each person on their week's dreams. There would be laughter when I told of yet another dirty swimming-pool dream or when Sarah described the feasts which were regularly laid before her (she is the one with eating problems, if you remember). We gradually became familiar with each other's dream-worlds and were able to spot things which the individual dreamer had missed in his own dreams. We would discuss problems of recall and recording and share newly discovered techniques. Then we would choose two or three individual dreams to work on in detail. We often used Gestalt, but we also tried out all the methods listed at the end of this chapter.

After a few weeks of work we each noticed that there were themes coming up in our dreams which were also being played out in our daily lives. For instance, Julie connected a figure in her dreams, whom she called "the wimp", with her passive and lazy behaviour in certain situations in her waking life; I noticed how I allowed myself to be intimidated by "bully-boys" in my dreams and also allowed myself to be bullied in my waking life, only in a much more subtle way. Sarah encountered food and piles of it whether asleep or awake, while Gerry dreamed of having to overcome obstacles, and there were certainly plenty of serious ones obstructing his path during the day. We decided to explore these themes via dream-work, trying out different attitudes and outcomes, and, if we found a new attitude which worked better than the old one, we would try it out in parallel situations in the outside world. We paid particular attention to the feeling-quality associated with the negative pattern in our dreams, so that we would recognise it when it came up in waking life and would be able to intervene and possibly change our habitual response to it. This was difficult! In fact, it turned out to be a very long-term piece of work – some of us found that we got no "results" till months or years later.

In my own case, there was a period of a few weeks when I kept dreaming about these "naughty boys" or "thugs" who would attack me in the street, steal my money or mock me. In the dream-group I got the chance to "become" these boys and see things from their point of view. It turned out that they were mischievous pranksters who had nothing better to do with their energy than cause trouble. My well-behaved, sober, hard-working self was an ideal target for their mischief. I had then to realise that I was not using up all my energy in my work, and that the spare stuff was feeding these rascals. The only way I could stop their attacks would be to find a way of using that energy properly. Now, *gradually* I learnt to do that, but it was not a simple matter. The energy had a large *physical* component and so I had to wake up my physical self in order to use it. I became keen on dance and drama, and that helped, but still I had the problem of approaching things with a rather rigid, presbyterian work ethic and not finding it easy to relax and allow the "trickster" side of myself to play. (I eventually solved that problem by *marrying* a mischievous trickster figure, who does not let me get away with being over-disciplined and holier than thou!)

So did the dream-work eventually work? I believe it did: it *triggered* a slow process of change in me, which accomplished itself over years – and which is still going on. I do not dream of the bully-boys any more, and am much better at sticking up for myself at home and work. When I catch myself in the act of being intimidated by a group of drunken lads or a domineering boss at work, I remind myself that *I* am feeding their power over me and *I* can choose to stop feeding them. Then they have no power over me.

So, we found that dream-work does not always produce quick, spectacular results, and even in cases when it does, you may find that you have to fight the same battle over and over again. This was the case with work Julie did on her negative feelings about her mother.

Julie did not get on with her mother. She shut her out of her life, thought of her as a silly old woman, and was utterly exasperated by her behaviour on the rare occasions when they met. Then she dreamed that she was at a dream-group meeting and her mother was there saying "Oh I don't know about all this – I think a woman's place is in the home." Julie was thinking "you silly lady", but at the same time another voice in the dream was saying "She's paid her dues and she's entitled to exist."

Julie says that "becoming" her mother in Gestalt exercises was interesting, but that what *really* helped was the general discussion about mothers which followed our work with her on this dream. This prompted her to read a book on the archetype of the mother and to realise that she had made a *decision* at some point about her mother, so that *whatever* she said, Julie would automatically dismiss it. Now, following the example of the dialogues she had had with her "dream-mother" in the group, she began to *listen* to her mother in waking life, and to argue with her. If her mum said "A woman's place is in the home", Julie would ask her "Why?" instead of ignoring her words and classifying her as pathologically silly!

For a year or so Julie's attitude towards her mother was transformed and their relationship improved accordingly. But then Julie became pregnant and she found herself "taking against" her mother again. Her dreams faithfully reflected what was going on: she had three about her mother – in the first, her mum was mad, in the second pathetic and in the third angry. In each, Julie "stood up" to her mother. It would seem that being on the point of becoming a mother herself had re-awakened her aggressive feelings towards her own mother. But, this time round, there was a significant difference in Julie's attitude: she had angry *expressive* dreams, and in her waking life she also *expressed* her anger towards her mother. The result is that, although her relationship with her mother is difficult, it *is* a real, communicative human relationship. Here's what Julie herself says about the situation:

Before, I hated her for doing certain things and said nothing. Now I say what I feel and feel awful for five minutes, but she stops doing it and next time round there's one thing less on the agenda to feel angry about. You've got to face it and sort it out. It's tough for my mum, but then I think 'that's life' – I'm not here to protect her from herself. And hopefully – I tell you it's a long process – we might be able to come to some arrangement where we enjoy each other's company. But anyway I feel better, more at ease with myself.

Julie also adds, commenting on her dreams in general:

I notice that I've been *intervening* a lot more in my dreams. I have far fewer *passive* dreams, where I'm an observer. And anxiety dreams? I'm not bothered. I had one where I missed the plane, lost my passport, and I thought 'well, to hell with it, I'll stay here!'

Julie's experience gives a flavour of the kind of personal work we did in the group, but we also devoted time to the development of the faculty of Active Imagination. The idea was to learn to observe the mind's image-producing faculty, while wide awake. To do this, Lynne and I introduced the group to *guided visualisation*.

In this exercise all the members of the group shut their eyes and the leader takes them on an imaginary journey. The leader gives the outline and each individual fills in the details for himself. Afterwards, everyone reports back on what he or she has seen and experienced. To give you an idea of how this works I will write out the instructions I gave the group in our first guided journey, and you can try it yourself, stopping each time I write *PAUSE* to follow the instructions in your imagination and write down what you see. Don't try too hard, just treat the exercise as an enjoyable piece of daydreaming and get down what you see, quickly, without criticising or censoring yourself. Ready? OK, let's begin:

You are walking along a road in the outskirts of a city, heading towards the centre. What is the weather like? What sort of buildings can you see? Are there any people around?

PAUSE

You are near the centre now, and you are looking for a certain house. It is just around the corner. . . . What does it look like? Is it familiar to you, or strange? How do you feel about going in?

PAUSE

Enter the house. What is the hallway like? Take some time to explore the house. What are the furniture, the decor like? Is there anyone else in the house? How do you feel?

PAUSE

Is there a room in the house that you have not yet explored? Maybe the basement, the attic, the kitchen? Go there. Do you like the room? If there is anyone else there, you may talk to them, ask them a question. What normally goes on in this room?

PAUSE

You are about to leave the house. On the way out you notice a book lying by the door. Pick it up. Does it have a title? A picture on the cover? Open it at random. What do you see?

PAUSE

Open the front door and leave the house. Start walking out of town again. In a moment you are coming back to the room in Lynne's house in Manchester. When you're ready, feel the weight of your body in the chair, open your eyes and bring your attention back into this room.

(At this point, if I were doing the exercise with a group, I would look around and check that nobody looks "spaced out". If anyone is still a bit dreamy I would get them to stamp their feet and walk about until they felt absolutely woken up.)

So how did you find the journey? Was it easy to visualise your surroundings or difficult? Don't worry if it was hard: some people's imagination is not primarily visual. Maybe you heard or smelt something, or simply were aware of a certain atmosphere. Did the whole thing turn into an adventure or a melodrama? If so, you were trying too hard and probably using your conscious mind too much. Did you see or experience anything of personal significance during the journey? For instance, did you meet someone and talk with them? Or see something written in the book which had meaning for you? If so, meditate on it by all means, but don't attach too much importance to it – the point of this exercise is not so much to explore the individual psyche as to practise receiving images as they well up, without interfering with the process by commenting and criticising.

When the exercise is done in a group it is interesting to see how much difference and how much similarity there is in what people see. We found that several of us "saw" the same sort of house, but that otherwise the details were different for each person. In subsequent meetings we went back to the house and found a room in it that was ours. We visualised it in detail, and then we visualised each other in it and noticed what each of us was wearing and doing. There was a meal laid out for us, and something else in the room left there especially for us. Each of us had to try to discern what it was. Afterwards we compared notes.

Although the room was different for each of us, there was one thing that we all noticed – it had a warm and welcoming feel to it. James, the writer, noticed that all of the group had "glowing eyes" and that each of us was dressed in a different colour – Lynne, red; myself, silver; and Mary (the computer programmer) in perspex! Mary, on the other hand, saw Lynne warming her bottom at the fire and busied herself finding a lid for the dish of new potatoes! But the differences didn't matter – we were learning to "see" for ourselves, to tell the difference between conscious fantasy and true Active Imagination. Each person saw the room according to his or her gifts and personality, but it was nevertheless the same room, a room where we could meet in the imagination.

We re-visited the room many times, and each time the atmosphere in it was different, and we saw each other differently. Sometimes, instead of reporting back afterwards, we took it in turns to tell what we were seeing while we were seeing it, so that we could all try to share the vision. Sometimes we made forays outside the house, into the surrounding countryside, and finally we arranged for each of us to have an "adventure" in the land outside the house, followed and supported by the rest of the group.

Of course, it is possible to use the principles of guided visualisation for completely different ends. Therapists use it to investigate the psychic landscapes of their clients, so that a flooded meadow or a gloomy basement would be used as a diagnostic clue. Our group was not therapeutic in essence, but exploratory.

The practice of guided visualisation over a period of months developed in us all the ability to home in on a particular scene from a dream and examine its content in detail. We could hold it in our minds clearly enough to explore and even expand it in any direction that seemed fruitful. We usually found that this process produced a *distillation* of whatever quality or atmosphere lay at the heart of the dream. Once we had discovered this *essence* it could be explored in itself, and was often the source of a very special sort of energy. Let me give an example of what I mean.

I had a dream in which I ended up, with a mysterious,

kindly man, in a room high up in an apartment block in India. It was a beautiful room, but rather dusty and neglected. While the man went out to work, I set about examining it. I found that the dust was the remains of dead spiders which still had the power to sting me when I touched them. I was curious about this dream because it held a vague quality of happiness and promise which I could not quite put my finger on.

In the group Lynne led me through a guided visualisation in which I explored the room thoroughly. I became aware of an atmosphere of stillness which was both calming and thrilling; the air seemed to be saturated with a very fine sort of energy, like the air you breathe at the seaside on a bright frosty day, but there were all those dead spiders lurking in the corners of the window frames and at the back of the shelves. . . . Lynne suggested I took a damp cloth and cleared them up, which I did. Then I set about cleaning and decorating the room. I hung a beautiful embroidery of animals in a forest (from another dream!) on one wall; I added a window which looked out over the sea, just visible in the distance; I placed an old, leather-topped desk in the bay window which overlooked the street, and a chaise-longue in the other alcove. When Lynne asked me what I was going to do in the room I said "write". I did not feel lonely there because I could see all the activity down in the street, and it was warm from the sun which slanted in through one of the windows, through gauzy curtains.

After that, whenever I sat down in the morning to write, I would go to that room in my imagination, wander round it looking down into the street, sit at the desk and just sense the quality of thrilling stillness in the air. It always put me in the right frame of mind to start writing. It was a creative place which I had discovered inside me, and with Lynne's help, I had become conscious of it, so that I could have access to it at any time I needed. Without dream-work I would not have known that it existed.

Everyone has this kind of place inside them, if they will only look for it. For some people it might be outside on a mountain-top, or in the cabin of a boat. Or you might find that a dream-image of a café in an East-European railway station carries a special atmosphere for you. Finding this place is something which does not have to be done in a group – you could do it on your own or with a friend – but remember, once you've found the place, keep going there and using it, otherwise it may fall into disrepair!

A dream-scene or place can also be the starting point for a different sort of dream-work. You can choose to concentrate on a scene which is full of tension and unresolved conflict, perhaps a crisis point. In this case you will need to draw or paint the scene in as much detail as possible. Don't worry if you're not an artist – after all, no-one is going to see the picture except you! (If you really can't bring yourself to draw, then write down a description of the scene, making it as accurate and vivid as you can.) Leave your work for a day or two, and then return and develop your "story" further. What happens now will not necessarily have anything to do with the original dream: use the "transcendent function", watch what arises from your unconscious but don't be ruled by it – try to get a balance between what the unconscious throws up and what your ego finds right. Let them argue it out if necessary in a dialogue. Then draw or paint another picture which expresses the new development. Come back to it in a few days and repeat the process, until you have a series of pictures which tell a story. Don't rush it – it does not matter if the completion of the work takes months. Stand back at various points and ask yourself what your series of pictures or your narrative (if you still can't bring yourself to draw!) says about you. Is it sentimental and sickly? In which case are you inhibiting the flow of fresher, more vigorous images from your unconscious? Is it weird and psychodelic? In which case do you have a stereotyped idea of what lies in the unconscious, gleaned from

71

drug-inspired comics? However, *don't judge yourself*! Just observe and consider: this is *your* story, you are its "onlie begetter". If you don't like it you can change it – unless you are still too attached to the negative patterns you create . . .

All these suggestions for things to do in a dream-group may not mean a great deal to you until you start your own and see how it develops. You may find that you want to concentrate on therapeutic work, or you may want to experiment with using dreams as a source of inspiration for other work – say, poetry or drama. But whatever your bias is, just one more hint before we move on: introduce some discipline into the group quite early on. If you impose a few simple rules, such as "Be punctual", "Pay attention when other people are working on their dreams", "Be accurate and brief when reporting on your dreams", you will find you save energy and discourage selfishness. And it is a good idea to take it in turns to work on your dreams – that way no-one can hog the time and the limelight! Remember, the *most difficult* hurdle is getting people to *remember* their dreams; once you've cracked that one, you're well on the way to making a relationship with the unconscious. Good luck and sweet dreams!

Dream-work Techniques

1) REMEMBERING AND RECORDING

Keep pen and paper (or cassette recorder) by bed, plus torch if putting on the light would wake someone. Repeat to yourself before going to sleep your intention to remember your dreams. Write down dreams *immediately* on waking, either straight into your dream-diary, or onto paper from which you will copy into the diary later in the day. (This is so that patterns and themes can be spotted over a period.) Note all the details you can remember, plus any *feelings* the dream evoked. Then add any associations or ideas which occur to you immediately, in relation to the dream. (Other things can be added later as they come to mind.)

Use something as a *cue* to jog your memory; for example, have a glass of water by the bed, drink half of it before going to sleep, and tell yourself that when you see it in the morning you will remember your dreams.

If you do not have to get up straightaway, lie in bed with your eyes shut and trawl for any stray images which could be the *hook* with which you can drag back the rest of a dream. For instance, if someone is on your mind on waking, it could be that you have dreamed of him. Shift yourself into the various positions you might have slept in during the night – this may help you to remember the dream you had while in that position.

Paying attention to your dreams and doing work on them will help you recall more dreams.

Going through your day *backwards* (exactly as if you were watching a film run backwards) before sleeping can clear the mind and get the digestive process going, so that not only will you recall your dreams better, but they may be more interesting because you have already *consciously* done some of the mind's donkey-work.

2) INCUBATION (asking for a dream to answer a question or help throw light on a problem)

Put the question very clearly to the dreaming power within you before you go to sleep. Write it down, or put it into a prayer, or make up a little ritual to frame the request (depending on what your attitude to dreams, religion and magic is). You could also follow some of the practices which the ancient Greeks undertook: purify yourself by taking a bath and putting on clean night-clothes, or sleep in a different bed, in a room which has been specially cleaned and prepared. Or you could collect herbs and put them in a muslin bundle under your pillow. The object of all these preparations is to signal to your unconscious mind that you are really prepared to listen to what it has to say.

Remember that the "answer" may not come in the form you expect it to, or may not come at all, though that may be a kind of answer too. Incubation is really a form of prayer, and a humble and open attitude is a prerequisite for success. On the other hand, never accept "instructions" from a dream which go against your own moral principles. (But don't confuse morality with a narrow sort of common sense – an idea which initially seems daft may still prove a wise one!) Even if a dream seems strongly to suggest a certain course of action, you still have to decide, with your waking mind, whether you want to take it or not!

You can also use this technique to ask for clarification of another dream which you have not been able to understand. For example, "Please, dreams, the image of the black cat with the envelope in its mouth still foxes me – can you put it another way so that I can grasp the meaning?"

3) GESTALT

See Chapter 3.

4) ACTIVE IMAGINATION (including dream re-entry, finding a place, making up a story, and other sorts of dream-manipulation done while awake)

See Chapters 3 and 4.

5) GUIDED VISUALISATION

See Chapter 4.

6) THINKING ABOUT DREAM THEORY

This might not sound as exciting as the other techniques, but it is an excellent corrective to the vagueness and woolly-mindedness which can creep into dream-groups.

Either start with a talk from an outside person (such as a doctor who knows about the physiology of dreaming, or a psychoanalyst who uses dreams in her work – or even a meditator who believes dreams are a lowly thing), *or* set a topic such as "What is a dream?" or "Are there different kinds of dreams?" and discuss it. Do not take anything you read about dreams as "gospel"; examine it for yourself, test it out against your experience. Appoint a chairman to cut through meanderings and bring people back to the point.

Some people will not like this exercise and they are exactly the kind of people who most need to do it. An intellectual structure for thinking about dreams is not counter-creative: it helps you organise your thoughts and experiences so that energy is not wasted in confusion. And of course it is only a map which can be thrown away if it is no longer useful.

7) MAKING A DREAM OBJECT

If something appears in a dream which particularly strikes you or moves you (e.g. a tapestry, a bowl, a geometric pattern), you can make a replica of it in your waking life. The process of making it and the contemplation or use of it afterwards will tell you more about what it "means" than analysis. In the dream-group Gerry told us about one of his "obstacle" dreams in which a piece of wood played a big (obstructive!) part. We suggested that he find a piece of wood and make it into something, to try to transform it into something positive. He made a paperweight out of a log, and, of course, every time he looks at it he is reminded of his dream-task.

Alternatively, maybe something is cropping up in your dreams which is bothering you – say, you are invited to grand functions but have nothing to wear. In this case you could make a beautiful dress in waking life, and you would then be prepared for your dream parties!

A variation on this would be to do something in waking life suggested by a dream; for instance, if you dream of driving badly and you can't drive, learn to drive. Or try relating dream-themes and problems to similar themes and problems in waking life (see the examples on page 63).

Be careful though! Don't set yourself Herculean tasks which probably come from the bossy "topdog" in you, and don't become obsessive about achieving them. All dream-work should be done with a light touch and persistence, not with a heavy, self-punishing hand.

8) WORKING WITH SYMBOLS

Symbol interpretation is hedged around with traps for the unwary. I feel it is usually better to try out other methods of understanding a dream first, before trying to "interpret" symbols. This is because to translate or interpret a symbol is to fix it and to remove some of its numinous, living quality. What the symbol stands for or points to may be a delicate, multi-faceted reality which will melt away if you handle it roughly. A symbol is a point of meaning – if you take away anything which is part of it, the meaning may collapse. Then comes that familiar feeling of frustration and "not getting anywhere". So remember, "Tread softly, for you are treading on your own dreams!"

However, there are other ways of tackling symbols apart from interpreting them, and these protect their integrity as well as exposing their meaning. The first is:

Associations
Write down or tell someone all the associations the symbol has for you, whether they be personal (the bath in your dream reminds you of the old one in your mother's cellar), verbal (you looked up the word "bathetic" yesterday and were surprised to see that it existed), mythological (the bath is a symbol of purification). Or perhaps the bath is a funny shape – in fact it looks more like a pram. Or maybe the city

of Bath has significance for you. . . . If any of the associations come from the few days before the dream, then they may be more reliable pointers – say, if you had just received a postcard from your brother in Bath saying he was getting married.

The next thing is to ask whether any of these associations have *meaning* for you. Do they relate to what is preoccupying or bothering you at the moment? Do they set off any interesting trains of thought? Do they make you feel a particular emotion? Remember, the symbol *may* contain several layers of meaning.

This exercise may be enough to open up the dream for you. You may feel you are stumbling onto the right path. If not, try this:

Symbol immersion (as described by Strephon Kaplan Williams)
Just hold the image in your mind and dwell on it. Don't bore into it with your attention; just hold it lightly, and, if your attention strays, bring it gently back. Notice what feelings, qualities, ideas come up, but *don't* follow trains of association.

If the same symbol keeps cropping up, and it is still foxing you, try:

Symbol research and brainstorming
The idea here is to feed as many ideas as you can into your mind. Go to the library and look up your symbol in encyclopaedias of mythology, art books, etc. Then have a brainstorming session in the group where everyone throws in their ideas and contributes bits of knowledge. People's different interests and specialities give them different bits of the jigsaw: an astrologer has access to a complete symbolic system rich in resonances and correspondences; a Greek scholar will know all about the private lives of the minor

77

godlings; on the other hand, the OAP who watches all the soaps on TV may know as much about mythology as anyone . . .

Dream dictionaries give you fairly precise definitions of the meaning of symbols. There is often some truth in these definitions, and these books can be useful if used carefully as inspiration rather than dogma. Tom Chetwynd's *Dictionary for Dreamers* (a rather superior example of the genre) says under the heading "car":

Sexual drives; the virility and energy of the man. The impulse to get away, leave home or move on, 'get a move on' in any other way. (40)

I used to dream of being in a car, and not knowing how to drive it properly. Then I took lessons and passed my test and the dreams stopped. Now I am pretty sure those dreams were about not knowing how to handle certain sorts of energy, and learning to drive was a symbolic way of taking steps to learn how to control that energy and use it fruitfully. If I had tried to interpret the dreams in the light of Chetwynd's dictionary I might have led myself up the garden path, and not bothered to learn how to drive! However, to be fair, I can see that my "out of control" cars maybe did have something to do with the somewhat wayward "virility and energy" of the man I was going out with at the time, and of course, learning to drive did mean that I could "get a move on" with my life. So I can't condemn dream dictionaries out of hand, even though I would like to!

9) DREAM AS DRAMA (acting out your dreams)

This is an entertaining and effective exercise for reasonably extroverted people. You need a fairly large room to do it in, so you might need to hire a church hall for a night. Each person takes it in turn to be "director" and gets the others to play the parts of different elements and characters from

78

his dream. He must give accurate and quite detailed instructions so that his actors do what he wants and not what they think would be fun. He may play the part of himself in the dream or ask someone else to do it while he watches. Then there is a run-through where everyone acts out the dream. The director/dreamer can rehearse his cast as often as he likes until they get the quality that he is looking for. *Then* he may *change* the action or outcome of the dream, so that what is tragic becomes comic, or what is unresolved is resolved, or aggression sublimated gets expressed, and so on. Try to get people to do this seriously. If there is too much giggling and self-consciousness it won't work. If you are unsure about how to get people going on something like this, there are bound to be community theatre people in your area who would come along and help – and maybe enjoy the chance to work on a dream of their own. This exercise is particularly good for bringing out the *emotional* qualities of dreams.

Now the statutory word of warning: don't do it until you know all your group-members well and until you have done a fair amount of other work. It's not something to be done by someone in a fragile emotional state. It should be used to explore the dreams of people in a reasonably sound psychological condition, not to tackle serious neuroses or help people in distress. Those sorts of things should be left to the experts.

10) LIFE AS A DREAM

This could be set as homework for the group and reported on at the next week's meeting.

Take a chunk of your day – say, from leaving the house to go shopping until you get back home again – and think of it as a dream, which you will later remember and work on. Write the "dream" down and treat it like a real dream, looking for themes, symbols, etc, and doing some Gestalt or dialogue work on it, as seems appropriate.

I found this exercise, suggested in one of the "Seth" books, absolutely fascinating.

11) SYMBOL AND PERSON-COUNT

Make a list of all the symbols which crop up in your dreams over a period of time (minimum six months), and another list of people. Work out the number of times each symbol or person appears. This will clearly show what the major themes and preoccupations of your life are, and who or what is making the biggest impression on you.

12) LEARNING TO BE LUCID

This means: learning to "wake up" within a dream and know that you are dreaming. In this state many interesting experiments are possible. Details in Chapter 6.

Many more techniques for dream-work can be devised within your group, but if you need further inspiration try Ann Faraday or Strephon Kaplan Williams, or go back to the old masters like Freud and Jung. The coming chapters of this book can be used as material too. *Don't* work with dreams under the influence of alcohol or drugs, and watch out for emotional parasites who want to use your group for their own ends. On the funny side, however, if you advertise publicly for members, you may have some entertaining moments. A plump lady spiritualist honoured our group with her presence for a couple of weeks. Airily she explained to us that each night she was whisked away (in her astral body of course) to various far-flung spots throughout the solar system, where the secrets of the universe were imparted to her. "What kind of things have you found out?" I asked her eagerly. "Oh," she replied loftily, "I never *remember* what they tell me!"

What a creative dreamer that lady could have been, if only she had been able to remember!

Creative Dreaming

As a man is, so he sees. (41)

"Creativity" is a word which has been over-used to the point that its real meaning has almost disappeared. It sounds good, it sounds exciting, but what is it? My Chambers dictionary says that "create" means "to bring forth, to produce", and, when used of God, "to cause to exist", especially "to form out of nothing". If we look at the first meaning, we are all "bringing forth" all the time, creating words and actions and emotions. In this sense human beings are basically creative even when they are not trying to be. But if we extend the meaning to include the second definition ("to cause to exist, to form out of nothing"), we are looking at man not as he is but as he aspires to be, as he is at his best – man in the image of God, forming something new out of nothing and making the unknown known by giving it a form.

Bearing these two levels of creativity in mind, let's look at dreams. Are dreams *in themselves* creative? In the first sense, yes, they are endlessly creative. Watch your mind as you drift off to sleep and notice how, at a certain point, as waking consciousness begins to fade, the image-manufacturers get to work, spinning a web of fantasy from every association that comes up. (It is difficult to watch this going on because you will tend to fall asleep, but if you persist you should be able to get a glimpse of the process before you drop off!) However, the chains and webs spun by the playful mind in this state are not usually particularly interesting or significant. The mind is not being "creative" in the second sense, it is not bringing anything new into being, simply playing about with old associations.

Similarly I would say that most dreams, while often entertaining and intriguing, are not actually creative. They can be very useful, and they can be worked on or with, as we have seen in previous chapters, to achieve therapeutic or developmental goals. But, if you want to go further than that and venture into the unknown, to the place from which "new" things arise, then you have to face the fact that dreams on their own do not constitute a way of contacting the creative within you. Further investigations are called for.

How come then, you may ask, that so many artists, writers and scientists have used dreams to throw up new themes, techniques and ideas, and to solve knotty intellectual problems? We will go into this in detail in a moment, but first let it be said that dreams "worked" for these people because they had put in so much intensive and conscious work themselves first. They had probably spent hours and days sitting with a blank page in front of them, struggling to find a solution to their problem. It is as if the conscious mind has been battering away at the gates of the besieged citadel, which is the unconscious mind, which only surrenders and gives up its treasure at night, after the battery is over. Thus, while dreams are not a short-cut to creativity for a lazy mind, they certainly can be a source of inspiration and guidance for an active and disciplined one.

However, there is evidence which contradicts all that. I have come across individuals who have fascinating and creative dreams without doing any "work" beforehand, and by that I mean the kind of dreams which are fascinating to others as well as to the dreamer. Jennifer is such a person. She is an intelligent woman in her thirties who lives alone and works in local government. She does not describe herself as a "creative" person and admits that her job is rather dull. But, about eighteen months ago, she began to have a particularly vivid series of dreams which interested her because "they were lucid and exciting in the way that good adventure stories are". She began to write down the dreams in the morning and found that this helped her to remember them more clearly. She says:

Then I found that I was thinking about the dreams as stories, wondering how they might turn out. It surprised me to find bits of these dreams popping up again in later dreams and so I was able to serialise them! The more I thought about them the more they would come!

Here is Jennifer's account of the most interesting of her dream-series:

It began with the eruption of a volcano in a peasant farming region of Europe where I was a fourteen-year-old girl working on the high slopes with a collective from my village. I was struck on the head and lost consciousness. I woke inside a huge metal transporter and was delirious and sick along with the other inhabitants of the vehicle. When the transporter stopped we were herded out by our "rescuers" who wore breathing apparatus and assumed the dress of soldiers, and were driven by them ever upwards into a mountainous region where all sorts of weird and frightening events took place. A few people died or disappeared on the way.

After many events we were brought to a plateau where a big walled city stood which was governed by a King and Queen. The King was a lecherous, self-indulgent and unpleasant character, whereas the Queen was good and kind and blue! She was entirely blue – hair, face, the lot. When I first saw her in the dream it was a big shock, I can tell you!

The Queen enrolled me as a trainee attendant and I then began a new life with a bunch of other girls. We were privileged and well-educated and were being taught the local wisdom of survival on this new planet – for it was not earth. I was told that I had been saved from death on earth and could not go back there. The destinies of this planet and earth, however, were interconnected in a way I did not fully understand, but had something to do with the periodic rituals that were performed by the Queen and her attendants.

In the dream I never lost the idea that I could get back to earth and I decided to run away from the city and look for a way back.

In another dream I did run away and was recaptured twice. All these events took place over two years of my life in the dream. In the second recapture I was taken by a soldier and suffered my first sexual experience at the age of sixteen. Finally I did get away and spent some time travelling with an Indian woman. I settled in one far-flung region, a pleasant place full of gardens, got married and had a child. Nine years later I found my way back to the city and to the Queen under very different circumstances!

I am still dreaming bits of all this and have begun to write it down. I know how this story ends but there are a lot of gaps to be plugged so you'll just have to wait.

Even though this is an undressed-up account of Jennifer's dreams, scribbled down at my request, I think you will be able to see that these fragments are of quite a different order from the usual run of dreams. The story they tell is coherent, absorbing, resonant: the details given are not random or absurd but significant: they increase our involvement in the narrative. The account reads like the outline of a science fiction or fantasy novel, and, indeed, Jennifer is hoping to use the material in a work of fiction. But why does she dream like this?

I can only suggest that it may be because she has always enjoyed dreaming and paid her dreams a certain amount of attention, eventually to the point of writing them down and thinking about them while awake. As I have already said in a previous chapter, the unconscious responds positively to being paid attention and *in some cases* is willing to organise itself to fulfil a conscious command or wish.

Of course there may be many other reasons for Jennifer's creative dream-life, to do with her psychological state and her hidden aspirations, but those do not concern us here: the fact is that it *is* possible to dream coherently and inventively – and you do not have to be a fully paid up "creative" person to do so!

Another way in which dreams can be creative is in solving puzzles which fox the waking mind. American psychiatrist Morton Schatzman has been carrying out experiments to monitor this function of dreaming. In a magazine article (42), he describes how he set readers a mathematical problem and asked them to try solving it in their sleep.

They were to write in to him with the results. The problem was:

Using six line-segments of equal length, can you construct four equilateral triangles, such that the sides of the triangle are the same length as the segments?

Quite a few of his correspondents had dreams which contained the answer, or clues to it, always expressed in the characteristically metaphorical language of dreams. Thus a schoolgirl who had just taken her "A" level chemistry exam had this dream:

I was walking outside my old primary school gates and running my hand along the school railings. Suddenly six of the railings came together and formed a kind of wigwam, and I was lying outside it playing cowboys and indians.

My father appeared and said that I was too old for that sort of thing and that I had to go to a party. I don't know what happened to the party, but next I was sitting in an exam room feeling the usual pre-exam butterflies. My chemistry teacher's face appeared and said "109 degrees 28 minutes". (42)

In fact, the girl's dream provided the solution twice over: firstly in the idea of the wigwam, because the answer to the puzzle is to think in three dimensions instead of two and build the "line-segments" into a wigwam, which will contain four equilateral triangles; secondly in the words "109 degrees 28 minutes". Apparently this is the bond angle in certain molecules in which the carbon atom sits at the centre of a regular tetrahedron, and a tetrahedron is made up of four equilateral triangles . . .

Schatzman remarks that it seems as if there is a part of the dreamer's mind, which could be called "the knower", which "knows" the answer to the problem before he does. He also noticed that none of the dreamers who successfully solved the problem showed signs of using in their dreams the kind of logical or experimental thinking which one would tend to use if trying to solve the problem while awake. In a follow-up article (43) he points out, however, that it is easy to miss these disguised clues in your dreams;

they need to be hunted for and mulled over before they will yield their secret. The schoolgirl mentioned above did not *immediately* see that her dream held the answer to the problem: she had to turn the dream-material over in her waking mind before she saw the solution hidden in it. In other words, it is only if you expect to find solutions to puzzles and problems in dreams that you will find them . . .

There are many stories of scientists and other brain-workers who have found the missing piece of a mental jigsaw in a dream. The most famous and most quoted example is that of Kekulé, the chemist, who discovered the structure of the benzene molecule this way. He had been working hard on the problem for some time, but just could not see how his formula could make a chain molecule. Then he dozed off in front of the fire . . .

. . . the atoms gambolled in front of my eyes . . . my mind's eye, trained by repeated visions of the same sort, now distinguished larger forma-tions, of various shapes. Long chains . . . everything in the movement, twisting and turning like snakes. And look: what was that? One snake grabbed its own tail, and mockingly the shape whirled before my eyes. I awoke as if struck by lightning; this time again I spent the rest of the night working out the consequences. (44)

Kekulé worked out that the carbon atoms in benzene could bond together in a ring, with the hydrogen atoms clinging on round the edges. His dreaming mind had presented this insight to him as an image of a snake following its own tail. But perhaps the most important line in his account is: "my mind's eye, trained by repeated visions . . .". Kekulé only had his inspiring dream *because* he had focused repeatedly on his problem over a long period of time.

Elias Howe had been trying for years to invent a sewing-machine, but had been unsuccessful because he could not solve the problem of how the needle could work the thread in and out of the material without getting in a terrible tangle. He had of course been thinking of the usual sort of needle which has its eye in the blunt end. Then one night he dreamed that he had been captured by a savage tribe who threatened to spear him to death unless he invented a workable sewing-machine within twenty-four hours. As the deadline approached Howe sweated with fear, but no inspiration arrived to save him. Then the savages advanced to finish him off, spears lifted at the ready, and he saw that in the tip of each spear was a hole!

This was the breakthrough Howe needed, the conceptual shift which made his sewing-machine a viable notion, because, of course, if the thread is passed through the sharp end of the needle, it can form a lock-stitch which holds without the needle having to be taken round to the other side of the material. I say "of course" because I have had the benefit of using sewing-machines based on this principle, but I daresay Howe still had quite a bit of thinking to do before his dream inspiration led to a working model.

If scientists have found the dream state productive of intellectual insights, how much more have artists and writers found it an inspiration. We are not here so much concerned with writers such as Lewis Carroll who explored the delights and paradoxes of the dreaming consciousness in their work, as with individuals who *used* the dreaming *process* to conceive and compose works of art or literature. Robert Louis Stevenson was such a man: he trained his unconscious not only to produce good story-lines, but also to ensure that they would be marketable commodities which would make him money too!

But his dream-life started less happily. As a child he was tormented by nightmares. Referring to himself in the third person, he writes:

He was from a child an ardent and uncomfortable dreamer. When he had a touch of fever at night, and the room swelled and shrank, and his clothes, hanging on a nail, now loomed up instant to the bigness of a church, and now drew away into a horror of infinite distance and infinite littleness, the poor soul was very well aware of what must follow, and struggled hard against the approaches of that slumber which was the beginning of sorrows. . . . He seemed to himself to stand before the Great

White Throne; he was called, poor little devil, to recite some form of words, on which his destiny depended; his tongue stuck, his memory was blank, hell gaped for him; and he would awake, clinging to the curtain rod with his knees to his chin. (45)

Happily, as he grew older, his dreams lost their metaphysical terror and became more entertaining: he took long, eventful journeys to beautiful places; he watched stories unfold in the Georgian period of British history in which he "masqueraded . . . in a three-cornered hat and was much engaged with Jacobite conspiracy". Also he began to read in his dreams tales "so incredibly more vivid and moving than any printed book, that he has ever since been malcontent with literature". (46)

And then there seems to have been a transition, from being "at the mercy" of his dreams, whether they be terrifying or thrilling, to being, to some extent at least, in control of them. He had early stumbled upon the fact that the playfulness of the dreaming mind is very entertaining. (We have all had the experience of wanting to go to sleep again to finish off an intriguing dream from which we awakened too early.) But he also seems to have been able to inject his conscious will into the dreaming level to the extent that it would order and pattern what was happening there into a form palatable not only to the waking Stevenson but also to the "market forces". And this is rather like what shamans are trained to do – only in their case they must bring back what is useful and meaningful to their tribe, not a marketable tale to feed the family!

It would seem that Stevenson got the idea for his famous novel *Dr Jekyll and Mr Hyde* from a process very like the dream incubation mentioned in previous chapters:

For two days I went about racking my brains for a plot of any sort; and on the second night I dreamed the scene at the window, and a scene afterward split in two, in which Hyde, pursued for some crime, took the powder and underwent the change in the presence of his pursuers. All the rest was made awake, and consciously. . . . All that was given me was the matter of three scenes, and the central idea of a voluntary change becoming involuntary. (47)

Here is an important clue for us: Stevenson only dreamed the *germ* of a story. What magic substance did that germ contain which convinced him that it was the theme for which he had been waiting? Any writer or artist will know the answer to this question: the germ idea contains a charge of intense, thrilling energy; it is alive with a kind of super-aliveness, a super-reality which triggers the imagination into enthusiastic action. This "charge" seems to come from beyond the usual level of dreaming, it has a very fine, very numinous quality. One might almost say it carries a taste of heaven, a taste of that place where the act of creation is eternally going on . . . anyway, it is the mark of a true artist that he or she recognises this special quality and honours it by finding the kind of imaginative clothing which will do it justice. You find this quality in all sorts of literature, but it is easiest to spot in the best of fantasy writing – C.S. Lewis's *Voyage of the Dawntreader*, Charles Williams's *Descent into Hell*, and, on a higher level, Dante's *Inferno* or Blake's prophetic verse.

Many writers have found inspiration in their dreams, but it is much rarer to find individuals who have systematically explored the use of the dreaming faculty to produce works of art. Thomas De Quincey was a man obsessed with dreaming: sometimes he was expending so much of his energy in opium-induced dreams that he had not even the strength to write a few lines in answer to a letter. He suffered dreadfully from his addiction but his accurate and vivid account of his dream-adventures is exceptionally useful to us if we would study the relationship between dreaming and creativity.

It may be objected that De Quincey's dreams were not ordinary dreams but drug-induced ones. However, it is important to note that, before he took opium, he was already a vivid dreamer. He was also a brilliant and sensitive man, on whom all impressions, particularly harsh ones, impinged most powerfully. One of his biographers,

Grevel Lindop, writes of him that "he was moving towards a conscious development of the dreaming faculty . . .he deliberately explored fantasy, observing it like a film show". (48) Lindop also makes the point that opium is not *necessarily* a hallucinogenic drug, and only became so for De Quincey because he consciously cultivated and paid attention to his mental imagery.

In fact, De Quincey plunged more deeply and recklessly into the world of dreams than any other British writer had before him: he discovered and explored new territories into which writers of horror stories and fantasies were not slow to venture. You can see traces of his "monstrous scenery" and "gloomy melancholy" in Lovecraft and Poe, and in the work of contemporary fantasists such as Alasdair Gray and Robert Irwin.

I seemed every night to descend, not metaphorically, but literally to descend, into chasms and sunless abysses, depths below depths, from which it seemed hopeless that I could ever reascend . . . the state of gloom which attended these gorgeous spectacles, amounting at least to utter darkness, as of some suicidal despondency, cannot be approached by words. (49)

Poor De Quincey had stumbled into the world of terrible energies which the shamans know, but, unlike them, he was not prepared or trained to face it. Nevertheless, he was not so overcome by its horrors that he could not report accurately what he saw there. He noticed, for instance, that in his dreams "the sense of space, and, in the end, the sense of time, were both powerfully affected" so that space expanded "to an extent of unutterable infinity", as did time, so that sometimes "I seemed to have lived for seventy or a hundred years in one night". He also noted that "the minutest incidents of childhood or forgotten scenes of later years, were often revived" so that he came to feel that "there is no such thing as forgetting possible to the mind". (50)

How did De Quincey manage to turn his dream

adventures and investigations into art? Many contemporary writers have offered us accounts of their drug-induced dreams and visions, and these are seldom of more than passing interest, but De Quincey was able to produce the kind of writing which stirs us and moves us and strikes us as illuminating and *true*. How did he manage to distil from the overwhelming proliferative chaos of his dreams an essence which touches us? How does he overcome the problem that other people's dreams are not usually of interest to us, however wild and full of exotic imagery they may be?

I think the answer may be that in his writing De Quincey was trying to find a way of integrating the harrowing and mind-threatening experiences of his dreams with his waking experience of life. One could guess that, had he not been able to do so, he might have gone mad. It is the sincerity and intensity of his efforts that enthrall the reader: we feel that he is all the time teetering on the brink of some extraordinary knowledge, some illumination which will make sense of it all. In fact, that knowledge never comes in one blinding flash, but it is present all the same: De Quincey did succeed in making what was potentially meaningless and chaotic, meaningful and beautiful. In this passage, from *Confessions of an English Opium Eater*, we see him struggling to come to terms with pain from an old wound: earlier in the book he has told us about a young prostitute called Ann, who befriended him and, he believed, saved him from death when he was starving and destitute in London. Much to his grief, he had lost touch with her and feared that she was dead. Seventeen years later he dreamed this dream, which, in its poignancy and clarity, is a classic of dream-art:

I thought that it was a Sunday morning in May, that it was Easter Sunday, and as yet very early in the morning. I was standing, as it seemed to me, at the door of my own cottage. Right before me lay the very scene which could really be commanded from that situation, but exalted, as was usual, and solemnised by the power of dreams. . . . I gazed upon the well-known scene, and I said aloud (as I thought) to myself, "It yet wants much of sun-rise; and it is Easter Sunday; and that is the day on which they celebrate the first-fruits of resurrection. I will walk abroad; old griefs shall be forgotten today; for the air is cool and still and the hills are high, and stretch away to heaven; and the forest glades are as quiet as the churchyard; and, with the dew, I can wash away the fever from my forehead, and then I shall be unhappy no longer." And I turned, as if to open my garden gate; and immediately I saw upon the left a scene far different; but which yet the power of dreams had reconciled into harmony with the other. The scene was an oriental one; and there also it was Easter Sunday, and very early in the morning. And at a vast distance was visible, as a stain upon the horizon, the domes and cupolas of a great city – an image or faint abstraction, caught perhaps in childhood from some picture of Jerusalem. And not a bow-shot from me, upon a stone, and shaded by Judean palms, there sat a woman; and I looked; and it was – Ann! She fixed her eyes upon me earnestly; and I said to her at length: "so then I have found you at last". I waited: but she answered me not a word. Her face was the same as when I saw it last, and yet again how different! Seventeen years ago, when the lamplight fell upon her face, as for the first time I kissed her lips (lips, Ann, that to me were not polluted) her eyes were streaming with tears; the tears were now wiped away; she seemed more beautiful than she was at that time, but in all other points the same, and not older. Her looks were tranquil, but with an unusual solemnity of expression; and I now gazed upon her with awe, but suddenly her countenance grew dim, and turning to the mountains I perceived vapours rolling between us; in a moment all had vanished; thick darkness came on; and in the twinkling of an eye, I was far away from mountains, and by lamplight in Oxford Street, walking again with Ann – just as we walked seventeen years before, when we were both children. (51)

This is a remarkable passage because, while it is very true to the logic and feeling-quality of dreams (sudden switches of location, powerful emotional atmosphere, time-jumps), it is also very moving. De Quincey has managed to get us to accept the dream as a *real experience*, which affected and changed him just as a waking event would have done. Perhaps we recognise that state of heightened, almost sacred emotion from our own dreams: we certainly know that poignant sense of loss and the joy of reunion with someone long dead or long missed.

But what can the ordinary dreamer learn from De

Quincey's researches into dreaming? Experimenting with drugs is always a dangerous practice, as De Quincey found out, and in individuals of unstable mind can lead to dissociation and psychosis. However, some of De Quincey's techniques are definitely worth adopting. The first is his steady application of the power of observation: even when his dreams are reaching new peaks of horror and grotesquery, he is still watching and recording and is able to put down on paper the finest, most subtle details. The second is his experimental attitude; he treats the world of dreams as an unknown continent which he is painfully exploring, and he takes the responsibilities of pioneering seriously. Lastly he is an indefatigable pattern-seeker: he does not kill his dreams with analysis, but he always notices if some particular piece of imagery comes from childhood or from a moment of heightened emotion later on in his life. In this way he builds up a map of his own psychic landscape. It is sad that his landscape should have been such a sombre one. Ours need not be!

De Quincey's opium habit weakened the barrier which normally separates the waking from the dreaming mind. Other writers have attempted to achieve the same state without drugs – William Blake being one of the more successful. He, too, found his way into the realm of titanic energies which the shamans and drug-experimenters know so well, but, perhaps because he was essentially a wholesome sort of man, it did not seem horrible to him. Awe-inspiring, terrifying, yes, but not grotesque, not hideous. This was the realm he described in his prophetic books. In *Jerusalem* he declared that his aim was:

To open the Eternal Worlds, to open the immortal eyes
Of man inwards into the worlds of Thought, into Eternity
Ever expanding in the Bosom of God, the Human Imagination. (52)

These prophetic books are not as easily readable as De Quincey's work, but that may be because Blake was trying to do a much more ambitious thing: in Milton's words, "to justify the ways of God to men". The truths he perceived were not communicable in normal poetic language: he had to find a new language in which to express them. How did he approach the task?

In his excellent book on Blake (53), S. Foster Damon tells us that Blake did a great deal of his writing at night, that he would wake up, get out of bed and scribble for hours, his dutiful wife sitting up to keep him company. Damon speculates that Blake found the state of semi-sleep, when the mind is alert and awake but still has access to the dreaming level, very conducive to composition.

In deep sleep the critical faculty vanishes entirely; but in the lighter forms of slumber, it is still powerful enough to keep the insistent logic of the mind from pushing itself to absurd extremes. At such moments then, the consciousness is at once Actor and Author, actually putting its adventures into words as they occur, and even controlling by this discipline of phrase-making those emotions that threaten an awakening. A whole pageant of brilliant visions is enacted, which the blissful dreamer struggles to make permanent in some verbal incarnation. (54)

Blake had been having visions since childhood (though he was always quite clear that they came out of his head, not out of the world) and so we may suppose that he had much freer access to the dreaming mind and the unconscious than most people. Because he was intelligent and creative, his dreams and visions tended to be meaningful and intelligible – like the shaman, he knew how to discern meaning in the play of great energies in the realm of the unknown. However, it must be said that, even if you know what all the characters stand for in the great myth which Blake created, *Jerusalem* is still a difficult poem. So it cannot be said that he was entirely successful in translating the dramas of his night-time visions into a form which the waking mind could understand. Nonetheless, if the poem is read, not with the grasping, logical mind to the fore, but in a receptive, dreamy state, its meaning somehow conveys itself anyway. Try this passage in that sort of frame of mind:

The banks of the Thames are clouded! The ancient porches of Albion
Darkened! they are drawn thro' unbounded space, scattered upon
the void in incoherent despair! Cambridge and Oxford and London
Are driven among the starry Wheels, rent away and dissipated
In Chasms and Abysses of sorrow, enlarg'd without dimension, terrible.
Albion's mountains run with blood, the cries of war and tumult
Resound into the unbounded night, every human perfection
Of mountain and river and city are small and withered and darkened.
Cam is a little stream! Ely is almost swallowed up!
Lincoln and Norwich stand trembling on the brink of Udan-Adan!
Wales and Scotland shrink themselves to the west and to the north!
Mourning for fear of the warriors in the vale of Entuthon-Benython
Jerusalem is scatter'd abroad like a cloud of smoke thro' nonentity.
Moab and Ammon and Amalek and Canaan and Egypt and Aram
Receive her little-ones for sacrifice and the delights of cruelty.

With what part of the mind do we understand "driven
among the starry Wheels"? What part of us responds to
those resounding lists of places-names, to that erratic,
galloping rhythm? I would suggest that this verse, with all
its exhilarating imagery, is received and understood by the
same part of the mind that manufactures dreams, and that
is why it is necessary to shift the level of your consciousness
in order to appreciate it. To Blake, the world of the
"Imagination" was as "real" as the physical world, but he
knew this was not so for most others. He wrote:

I know this World is a world of Imagination and Vision. I see Everything
I paint in this world, but everybody does not see alike. To the Eyes of a
Miser, a Guinea is more beautiful than the Sun, and a bag worn with the
use of money has more beautiful proportions than a vine filled with
Grapes. The Tree which moves some to tears of Joy is in the Eyes of
others only a Green thing which stands in the way. Some see nature all
Ridicule and Deformity, and by these I shall not regulate my
proportions; and some scarce see Nature at all. But to the Eyes of a man
of Imagination, Nature is Imagination itself. As a man is, so he sees. (55)

We might bear this in mind in relation to our own
aspirations to be creative dreamers. If our dreams are dull
or wickedly repetitive of the same old patterns, we might
need to look to ourselves and ask what we really are and

what we really care about – "as a man is, so he sees". It is only when petty personal obsessions and neuroses have been sorted out that we can begin to look in dreams for the reflection of a larger reality.

Many more painters than writers have managed to translate dream into art, perhaps because, in dreams, for most if not all of us, the visual sense is predominant. A list of dream-artists would include Bosch, Breughal, Cranach, Goya, Moreau, Rousseau, Redon, De Chirico, Chagall, Ernst, Samuel Palmer, Richard Dadd, Dali – and countless others. Each painter's dream-world has its own atmosphere: Chagall's is joyous, full of sensation and sudden gusty energy; Gustave Moreau's glittering, jewel-like interiors evoke a heavy eroticism; Samuel Palmer's innocent landscapes seem to be illuminated by a light from heaven; Redon captures the evanescent images (often half-formed and then rejected) which flit through our minds on the borders of sleep; Bosch and Breughal delineate our worst fantasies of punishment and retribution. And of course, in many cases, painters inject a quality of dreaming (such as super-real brightness or terrible desolation) into their work without even being conscious of what they are doing. For every artist worth his salt knows that *states* of mind can become *places*, and that landscapes can carry an emotional message as well if not better than a human face.

But the boldest explorers of the dream-world in art were the Surrealists, and the effect of what they saw and painted has been profound and long-lasting. A few nights ago I watched a lager advertisement on television which used dissociated fragments of imagery to create a weird, dream-like atmosphere. It was very entertaining, although I do not think it will make me want to drink lager! I could just imagine the whizz-kid director of the ad looking back to his first encounter with the Surrealists at art school – how it had opened up a whole Pandora's Box of possibilities for him! Even in a world jaded by the excesses of punk and commercialism, surrealist images still have the power to jar us and wake us up.

It all started when the young poet, André Breton, not long back from the horrors of the First World War, was about to fall asleep one day. As he lingered in the borderland between sleeping and waking a phrase "knocked at the window" (of his mind?). He thought the phrase was something like "a man is cut in half by the window", and it was accompanied by an image of the same thing. The phrase did not make sense and this was what excited him. He and his friends were struggling to escape from the tyranny of rationalism (a rationalism which had not in the least protected their generation from being sent off to fight a bloody war) and he hoped this might be the clue he was looking for, the clue which would reveal the true source of inspiration and the creative process.

This was in 1919 and, at about the same time, painter Max Ernst had a similar experience. He was looking at an illustrated catalogue, and:

There I found brought together such disparate elements of figuration that the sheer absurdity of this assemblage caused a sudden intensification of my visionary faculties and brought forth a hallucinating succession of contradictory images, double, triple and multiple images overlaying each other with the persistence and rapidity peculiar to memories and the visions of half-sleep. (56)

Both experiences happened on the threshold of sleep but while consciousness was not quite yet extinguished. Both Breton and Ernst saw the possibility of "stealing" imagery from that realm and carrying it back to full consciousness to become material for art. But they did not want the conscious mind to interfere and distort their treasure – they believed it came from a "higher reality". Breton wrote:

Surrealism rests on a belief in the higher reality of certain neglected forms of association, in the omnipotence of dream, in the disinterested play of thought. It tends to destroy other psychic mechanisms and to substitute itself for them in the solution of life's principal problems. (57)

97

As Breton's enthusiasm grew, he began to gather a group of friends together to perform experiments in hypnosis. One of their number, Robert Desnos, was able to talk, write and draw while in deep trance, and would answer questions put to him by the others. Louis Aragon recalls the scene in *Une Vague de Rêves*:

At the cafe, in the hubbub of voices, amid glaring lights and elbowing people, Robert Desnos has only to shut his eyes and he talks, amidst the rattle of beer-glasses and saucers, and the whole Ocean gives way with its prophetic crash and its mists adorned with long oriflammes. Let those who question this formidable sleeper goad him ever so little and out comes prediction and the tones of magic and revelation, the tones of Revolution, and those of the fanatic and the apostle. In other circumstances, were he to yield himself up to this delirium, he would become the leader of a religion, the founder of a city, the tribune of an uprisen people. (58)

Instead Desnos nearly became a murderer! One night, while in his trance, he seized a knife and threatened the poet, Paul Elouard. He was controlled in time, but this, and the fact that attendance at these sessions seemed to be having a deleterious effect on the participants – they were, according to Aragon, losing weight and getting into an irritated and nervous state – prompted Breton to call a halt. But the experiments had proved their point – there *was* another reality which could be reached in sleep and trance states, and in it was a rich vein of material which could be mined for poetry and painting.

Breton continued to pursue the surrealist vision with almost religious fervour. He wrote:

I believe in the future transmutation of those two seemingly contradictory states, dream and reality, into a sort of absolute reality, a surreality so to speak. I am looking forward to its consummation, certain that I shall never share in it, but death would matter little to me could I taste the joy it will yield ultimately. (59)

Surrealism never did lead its acolytes into this glorious promised land, but it did give outward and visible form to creatures and landscapes and concepts which had hitherto been hidden in the invisible world of the psyche. Even if you do not like surrealist art, you can hardly deny its power, to shock, to awaken, to fascinate. If, in the end, we feel there is something lacking in the Surrealists' vision, perhaps it is because they were drawn to the glamour of the changeable, chimeric realm of free association, rather than the more subtle and ordered landscapes inhabited by the dragons of meaning. They did not want to commit themselves to meaning – they wanted to stay free. In other words, they felt the unconscious was superior to the conscious, and were more interested in roaming around in the fields of the unconscious than in building bridges between it and consciousness. Above all, they were great rebels and adventurers.

It is immensely worthwhile for the student of dreams to spend time in art galleries and libraries contemplating the Surrealists' work, and to experiment with watching what arises in the mind on the brink of sleep and perhaps use it as material for some art form. In the same way, an individual intent on developing creatively may go through a startling and stimulating surrealist phase, where the contents of the unconscious are allowed to spill out unchecked and uncensored. But to go further, the aspirant has to recognise (as many of the Surrealists did not, being too attached to their own ideology) that there are levels beyond the levels of the unconscious to which the Surrealists had access. These very deep levels are not reached by fevered dredging for imagery, but they *can* be reached by meditation, or other spiritual practices. (They can also be reached by accident and by dreams of a rare and special sort – see Chapter 8.)

In meditation the meditator learns to watch the images and thoughts as they arise in the mind, but he trains himself not to be identified with them or attached to them, so that he may, in flashes at first, perceive what lies beyond them. What lies beyond them is the place from where they spring – a very creative place indeed! It has been described as a "rich void". Contact with this level can have the effect (amongst many others which need not concern us here) of organising and ordering the contents of the mind, calming it down in fact so that the still, small voice of inspiration is heard more clearly when it calls.

I have introduced the idea of meditation at this point because, if you are genuinely committed to the study of dreams, you may find you reach a point where dream-work has released a lot of energy in you and filled your head with a swarm of ideas, but where you feel somewhat confused by the mysterious workings of your own mind. At this stage, if you want to go further, the seeking out of a meditation teacher could be a good idea. Meditation will cut down the internal "noise" and introduce you to a kind of inner silence and stillness which will provide you with a safe vantage-point from which to view your dreams (and those of others!) It is emphatically not necessary to absorb any kind of religious dogma along with your meditation, and you do not have to be a "spiritual" sort of person to meditate. If you look, you will find schools and techniques of meditation which do not ask you to accept any kind of belief system along with them.

So far I have been talking about the kind of creative dreaming which solves scientific problems and inspires works of art, but most of us express our creativity in our day-to-day lives, at work and in our relationships with others. Can creative dreaming work for us? The answer, I believe, lies in the development of a relationship between the waking and the dreaming mind. The more we try, with the waking mind, to reach over the horizon of conscious-ness into the unknown realm of the unconscious, the more we get used to doing it, and the more open we become to inspiration, the kind of inspiration which breaks habits, weakens illusions, prompts spontaneous acts and makes us more active and less automatic in our living. But to do that, we have first to drop many prejudices and preconceptions about what is possible and what is not, about what counts as "experience" and what does not. If we do not do this, we will not learn anything or experience anything new.

This "commerce" between the waking and the dreaming mind can be encouraged in various ways. Many of the techniques suggested in the previous chapters (such as Active Imagination, doing a dream-task, and incubation) will begin to build up a two-way flow between the two camps. A relaxed and playful attitude is the best, plus an open mind. Becoming obsessively wrapped up in dreaming and working on your dreams, at the expense of paying attention to your waking life, is actually counter-productive. Seth has some wise observations to offer on the relationship between dreams and creativity:

Creativity connects waking and dreaming reality, and is in itself a threshold in which the waking and dreaming selves merge to form constructs that belong equally to each reality. You cannot begin to understand how you form the physical events of your lives unless you understand the connections between creativity, dreams, play and those events that form your waking hours. In one respect dreams are a kind of structured unconscious play. Your mind dreams in joyful pleasure at using itself, freed from the concerns of practical living. Dreams are the mind's free-play. The spontaneous activity, however, is at the same time training in the art of forming practical events. (60)

I think he is right – dreams *are* a kind of "structured unconscious play", and there is no creativity where there is no play and no experimentation. That is why the waking mind, usually wrapped up in anxious, end-orientated activity, needs to learn from the dreaming mind how to play, by exploiting the marvellous freedom of the imagination which knows no constraints of time or money or obligation. Seth comments:

You can travel in the dream state into levels of reality separate from your own. You can learn to use and experience time in new fashions. You can obtain knowledge from other portions of your own being, and tap the psyche's resources. You can improve the world in which you live, and the quality of life . . . (61)

It might be objected that in building up a relationship between the sleeping and dreaming selves we risk contaminating the conscious mind with the taint of the illogical, amoral dream-world. However, in fact, the aim is in the other direction – that the dream-world be ordered and organised under the direction of the conscious mind. This should not drain the magic out of dreams but begin to harness their power. Writing of the Senoi, Kilton Stewart says:

In the west the thinking we do while asleep usually remains on a muddled, childish or psychotic level because we do not respond to dreams as socially important and include dreaming in the educative process. (62)

The unconscious is like a vast desert which can never be tamed, but it can be cultivated in patches. Of course, there will always be a wild, impenetrable region "over there, beyond the far horizon", but we can make an oasis in the desert, or a tidal pool on the seashore (if you prefer the sea as a symbol of the unconscious). The oasis is part of the desert, the pool is part of the sea, and both are symbols of human creativity, and as Seth would say, "constructs that belong equally to each reality". Kilton Stewart has a good example not just of creative dreaming but of creative *use* of dreaming, which gives us a sense of the kind of power available to an individual who has built a bridge between the two realms.

Datu Bintung of Jelong had a dream which succeeded in breaking down the major social barriers in clothing and food habits between his group and the surrounding Chinese and Mohammedan colonies. This was accomplished chiefly through a dance which his dream prescribed. Only those who did his dance were required to change their food habits and wear new clothing, but the dance was so good that nearly all the Senoi along the border chose to do it. In this way the dream created social change in a democratic manner. (63)

Of course, you cannot really give people instructions on how to be creative, because the mark of a creative person is that he does not necessarily follow the rules he has been given and is capable of striking out alone and thinking for himself! So I will stop here and leave you with one question which you might like to consider in between thinking about your dreams: Who or what is it that dreams? Evidently sometimes the ego or waking consciousness is there because it remembers the dream, but what about the dreams which you do not remember? *Who* or *what* dreams them?

Chapter 6

Lucid Dreaming

Be awkward if it isn't a dream, won't it? (64)

What follows is one of the strangest dream-experiences I have ever had.

I was in a deep sleep one night when the door-bell rang. I woke up and rushed downstairs to find a young man at the door asking for my lodger. I told him that the lodger was not at home and went back to bed feeling jangled and irate. But I was very tired so I closed my eyes and settled down to sleep. Then suddenly I was in front of my bedroom window, looking out into the dark garden. I wasn't standing – in fact I appeared to be *floating* in the air! With a thrill I realised that I was dreaming. I decided to go outside, and somersaulted (the way you do off the side of the swimming-pool) over the window-sill and into the garden. As I hung there, looking around, I heard a voice say: "You'd better come back now", and I returned quickly to my body in bed. I woke up briefly at this point, but soon shut my eyes and almost immediately found myself somersaulting out into the garden again. I felt really pleased with myself and began to move about, feeling the night air cool on my skin. Then once again the voice warned me to "get back" and I complied.

Whether I woke again now I am not sure but I decided that, if I could do this trick a third time, I must find a way of establishing whether the garden was my real garden or a dream-garden which I was inventing. I somersaulted out once more and hung there in the dark. This time I heard the rhythmic sound of a lawn-mower coming from a neighbouring garden, and I knew triumphantly that I must be out in the real world. Feeling elated but exhausted by my experience I relapsed into ordinary sleep.

A "lucid" dream is a dream in which you know you are dreaming, and this one of mine nicely illustrates the kind of adventures and confusions you can fall into when your waking consciousness somehow manages to acquire a dream-body and enter your dreams! (In this case I believe it was the combination of physical tiredness and sudden arousal that produced a relaxed but alert state in me which was an ideal condition for lucidity.) First of all there's the shock (delightful or horrifying, depending on you) of realising that you are dreaming; then there's the thrill and exhilaration of being able to float or fly, plus the pleasure of exercising your mental faculties in a normal manner while asleep; and lastly there is the opportunity to experiment and investigate the environment of your dream. It is typical that although I thought I was using perfect waking logic in presuming that the sound of the lawn-mower meant I was in the real world, I was not in fact doing so! I had failed to realise that it was extremely improbable that any of my neighbours would be mowing their lawns by moonlight. So it would seem that I had invented not only the garden but the lawn-mower as "proof" that I was in the "real" world.

There is also the matter of the "wise voice" which seemed to be guiding and protecting me, but we will come back to that later when we know a little more about the principles and practice of lucid dreaming.

There are three stages of lucid dreaming. In the first the dreamer has some intimation, which may be fleeting, that she is dreaming, or may simply ask herself, "Am I dreaming?" but not come to any conclusion about this. Into this category we could also put those dreams in which we manipulate the rules of the dreaming world to our advantage, for this seems to suggest that some part of the mind at least is aware that it is not in the "real" world. Most of us have this sort of dream at some time.

The second stage, where the dreamer accepts the fact that she is dreaming and continues the dream in this knowledge, is rarer. This state seems to be precipitated by a variety of circumstances: for myself, I have noticed that either emotional distress or an unusual amount of mental activity during the day can produce lucid dreams – it is as if the mind cannot relinquish its obsessive activity even in sleep. Or it may be simply that something in the dream strikes you as incongruous – perhaps you meet a friend who is dead, or find yourself flying. When you realise that the friend cannot meet you or that you cannot fly, you deduce that you "must be dreaming".

At the third stage the dreamer not only knows she is dreaming but is able to exert some control over the dream, perhaps by experimenting with the objects she sees or going to visit places or people that interest her. Frederick Van Eeden was a diligent lucid dreamer who studied the phenomenon with meticulous attention.

On September 9 1904 I stood at a table before a window. On the table were different objects. I was perfectly aware that I was dreaming and I considered what sort of experiments I could make. I began by trying to break glass, by beating it with a stone. I put a small tablet of glass on two stones and struck it with another stone. Yet it would not break. Then I took a fine claret glass from the table and struck it with my fist, with all my might, at the same time reflecting how dangerous it would be to do this in waking life, yet the glass remained whole. But lo! When I looked again after some time, it was broken.

It broke all right, but a little too late, like an actor who misses his cue. This gave me a very curious impression of being in a fake-world, cleverly imitated but with small failures. (65)

Lucid dreaming is complementary to Active Imagination: whereas in the latter the waking mind has the upper hand, in the former the dreaming mind holds the balance of power, and will usually draw the dreamer away from his lucidity into an ordinary dreaming state. The work I have suggested in this book so far would provide good training for lucid dreaming: if it is carried out with any persistence, it will develop your powers of imagination and observation and also help you to keep alert and awake on that knife-edge between sleeping and waking. During lucid dreaming it would seem that one part of the mind is asleep while another is awake. What part is awake? The easy answer would be "the ego", but I do not believe that it is easy to enter into the lucid state while the ego is in a normal, fully operative state. From my own experience, lucid dreaming tends to occur only when some sort of stress, arousal or mental training has made the usual ego expand and relax. The "ego" present in lucid dreams is on the whole much more playful, open-minded, and indeed adventurous than the usual one.

If you are curious to experience this sort of dreaming, what can you do to encourage it, apart from the self-development exercises already mentioned in Chapter 4? The simplest trick is to tell yourself firmly before you go to sleep at night that you are going to wake up in your dreams and know that you are dreaming. You can reinforce this suggestion by deciding upon a trigger which will act as a reminder if it crops up in your dreaming; you could say to yourself that if you find yourself flying you will know you are dreaming; or that if you encounter a certain friend who is interested in dreaming, this will remind you that you should try to "wake up". These techniques may not work immediately, but if you keep at it steadily you will get results, although, on the whole, lucid dreaming seems to be a sporadic rather than a regular phenomenon for most people.

There are various factors which can stop lucid dreaming from continuing; the first of these is panic! Some people feel trapped and frightened when they realise they are dreaming and that the body they are in is the "dreaming body". But there is no reason to be frightened: in a lucid dream you have much more control than normal over what is happening and if anything untoward occurs it is within your power to change it. However, if you let any strong feeling such as fear swamp you, you will probably lose the lucidity, so it is best to remain calm and objective. Sexual desire is also a problem. Of course there is no real harm in indulging yourself in sexual adventures in dreams; the trouble is that, if you spend your energy that way, you will not have much left to channel into the steady awareness which is necessary to preserve the lucid state. Ann Faraday comments:

Sexual arousal in a lucid dream can lead to flying and out-of-the-body experiences when the sexual energy seems to flow up through the whole body; whereas on other occasions, when the energy stays around the genital area, an ordinary but intense sex dream occurs. Perhaps there is some connection with the old tradition which holds that sexual energies can be transmuted into other potentials when not confined to the energy-dissipating sex games of prestige and role-playing in our society. (66)

So, if panic and sexual fantasy can be avoided, the next problem is to stay lucid and not lapse into the usual dreaming state. A piece of advice which I have found useful is to look at your hands as soon as you realise you are dreaming. This immediately gives you a sense of having a body and of existing in space. It also seems to stabilise the lucid state for long enough to give you a chance to think of what you want to do next. This tip appears in Carlos Castaneda's books (more of him later) and was also passed on to me by a Sri Lankan friend who grew up in a family where dream-work was practised.

If you can maintain your lucidity and keep the dream environment reasonably stable, the next step is to decide what you want to do in your dreams. (It is a good idea to decide on this beforehand, otherwise you may spend valuable lucidity-time dithering!) You have a wide choice of objectives . . .

You can investigate the nature and qualities of the

dream-world as Van Eeden did, observe how the senses function there and how things look. Many people remark on the quality of the light in lucid dreams:

. . . electric light which had a slightly artificial quality – perhaps more mellow than electric light . . . (67)

Never had sea and sky and trees shone with such glamorous beauty; even the commonplace houses seemed alive and mystically beautiful. (68)

And many people have noticed that electric light switches do not seem to work normally in lucid dreams. I find that trying the light switch in my bedroom is one sure way of knowing whether I am dreaming or not!

Or you can exploit the physical freedom which is a feature of the lucid-dreaming state and fly or jump from high places.

I find myself at the edge of a frightful precipice, the mere sight of which makes me tremble; a sheer, or even overhanging cliff many hundred feet high. At the bottom are sometimes sharp rocks, sometimes houses and trees which look small in the distance. At the moment when I tremble and hold tight, the dream suddenly becomes conscious; I realise that I am dreaming, that all this is illusory and that I am in no real danger. Then, in order to see what will be the result of this decision, I make up my mind to throw myself into the abyss. I do so and I always arrive at the bottom without shock unless my fall ends in a delightful flight. (69)

An interesting feature of flying in dreams, as I have observed it (and this is true of flying in non-lucid dreams too), is that it is a very *physical* sensation. I generally notice a build-up of energy and excitement in the lower pelvic area (rather like sexual arousal but not so specific) which begins to spread upwards and, as it does so, lifts me off the ground. My whole body feels alive and tingling. It is a very pleasurable experience.

Or you can take a leaf out of the Senoi Indians' book and use your awareness that it is "only a dream" to come to terms with frightening figures or images. The great advantage of facing up to these sorts of figures and the fear they inspire, in a lucid dream, is that you quickly realise that, since you are not in your physical body, you cannot be hurt or killed – although in my experience it is possible to feel a kind of pain (only a pale imitation of the real thing, fortunately!) And perhaps more than any other kind of dreaming, lucid dreaming offers a perfect opportunity for conscious and unconscious mind to meet on equal terms: if you can avoid panic and maintain mental clarity, you can watch the mind's image-making faculty in action and actually do your dream-work *while* you are dreaming, instead of afterwards.

I still remember the joy I felt when I "woke up" in a dream containing a gang of vicious thugs of the type who had been harrying me regularly in my ordinary dreams at that time. They picked up rocks, intending to crush my skull, but the rocks just bounced off my head like papier-mâché, and the thugs retired growling. In another lucid dream I was shot at by Gestapo men while flying, and shouted gleefully at them, "You can't hurt me – my body is at home in bed!"

This might all sound like childish cops and robbers, but actually this dream-work was very beneficial for me: the thugs stopped turning up in my ordinary dreams – it was as if they had given up their bullying because it did not work any more. I also noticed that if I could recall that feeling of invulnerability in my waking life, it helped protect me from all sorts of psychological bullying by bosses, shop-assistants and bureaucrats!

Finally, you can address yourself to the various metaphysical questions which are thrown up by the strange phenomenon of lucid dreaming. For instance, if you meet someone in a dream, talk with him and even perhaps discuss the fact that you are dreaming, does this mean that he is also dreaming of you? In most cases this does not seem to be true – you can easily check by asking the person the next morning whether he had any interesting dreams in the night and, of course, if he dreamed of you he will probably mention it. (Although there is always the possibility that he did dream of you but has forgotten the dream!) However, there are cases where people seem to have made a genuine rendezvous in a lucid dream and remembered it the next day. Celia Greene gives a delightful example in her book on lucid dreaming.

A man called Oliver Fox, who was a great experimenter with dreams, had a friend, Elsie, who objected to his work on lucid dreaming, on religious grounds. But she was sufficiently nettled by Fox calling her an "ignoramus" in such matters to declare that she would appear to him that night in a dream. Fox reported:

Some time in the night, while it was still dark, I woke – but it was the False Awakening. . . . Suddenly there appeared a large, egg-shaped cloud of intensely brilliant blueish-white light. In the middle was Elsie, hair loose, and in her nightdress. She seemed perfectly solid as she stood by a chest of drawers near the right side of my bed. There she remained, regarding me with calm but sorrowful eyes, and running her fingers along the top and front side of a desk which stood on the drawers. She did not speak. (70)

The next day he encountered a very excited and triumphant Elsie, who said that she *had* come to him. Fox would not say a word of confirmation until she had given him a detailed description of some of the things in his room. Her account was very accurate – it seemed she really had visited him in her dream.

Which raises another question: is the world you see in a lucid dream always an invented world, or can it sometimes be the "real world"? In most cases, however vivid and sharply etched it seems, the environment of a lucid dream is clearly created by the dreaming mind. But again, there is the odd example, like the one above, which suggests that, very occasionally, the dreaming body sees and is seen in the "real" world. If you are intrigued by this issue, you can easily set up experiments for yourself, but do lay down the outlines of the experiment while awake or it may well be tainted with the wayward logic of the dreaming mind! You could, for example, decide to visit in your dream a place you have never seen in waking life (though beware that you have not seen a photograph of it or a TV programme about it). If you succeed, you should observe as many details as you can about the place, making notes as soon as you awake, and then make a visit to the place in waking life, to see whether it tallies with your dream-place at all.

Remember, also, that in lucid dreams you do not have to travel by conventional means. You can fly or teleport or merely "think" yourself to a place. Or you may decide that, in the dream, you will find a door and that on the other side of it is waiting the place or person you wish to see. When you open the door, the place or person should be there. I must warn you that this is easier said than done, and a great deal of practice is necessary before the right kind of balance is achieved between waking will and sleeping imagination. But it is such fun trying!

This is perhaps a good point to remind ourselves what an extraordinary phenomenon lucid dreaming is. In such a dream we feel ourselves to be in a body very like our usual one, except that it can rise up in the air and fly, and has hands which may glow with luminous light or extend far out from the body (my own experience – yours may be different); it can travel vast distances instantly, experience fierce sexual pleasure, and yet it cannot be injured by bullets or destroyed by fire or flood. It can however feel pain, and the heart within it is capable of beating fast with terror. The world it moves in may hold huge gothic castles and archetypal medieval cities, wherein you meet long-dead friends and engage in magical rituals; or you may find yourself inside a perfect replica of your own bedroom, the only thing to give it away as a replica being that when you look out of the window you see open fields instead of the tower blocks that are normally there!

There are two other interesting features of lucid dreaming which Celia Greene has spotted. The first is the humour latent in the situation. One of her anonymous subjects had this dream:

I found myself with X in a room at the other end of the corridor. I was telling him about the lucid dreams I had just had, and said suddenly as it occurred to me, "And of course *this* is a dream now." X said with an unhelpful smile, "Well, it *might* be. How do you know?" "Of course it is" I said and crossed to the window. This was heavily barred: outside were castle turrets and a long drop below to village roofs. "I'm going to fly," I said, and started to break off the bars. They broke as if made of a cross between chocolate and sealing-wax, and I threw the pieces down onto the roofs below. "Be awkward if it isn't a dream, won't it?" said X, who continued to stand by passively looking humorous. "It *is* a dream," I said firmly, though at the back of my mind I thought cautiously, "At the worst it couldn't be more than fifty pounds for tiles." (71)

Apart from the humour, it is interesting to note that people behave very much in character in lucid dreams – you rarely get the kind of bizarre fluctuations in personality which happen so often in ordinary dreams. I bet "X" in the above quotation was as sceptical and irritating in "real" life as he was in the dream!

The other feature Celia Greene points out is that people who have lucid dreams over a period of time notice a "learning effect"; that is, just as a child learns gradually how to manipulate the "real" world, so the lucid dreamer learns to function better and better in the dream-world. (I remember clearly, a few years ago, being taught to fly in my dreams, and then slowly gaining confidence within each dream of flying until I took it for granted that I could rise up at will and skim over seas and mountains.) And then there is the "wise voice" I mentioned at the beginning of this chapter. This voice has cropped up three or four times in lucid dreams and imparted something to me which, even when awake, I recognised as the kind of wisdom I was in dire need of at the time.

Here is an example: at the time of this dream I was anxiously looking forward to a party because I hoped to meet there a man I was rather keen on. This is the dream as I wrote it down at the time:

I am going to a party and X will be there. I am walking around and then I realise that I am dreaming. I panic and try to wake up but cannot, so I decide to go on dreaming. I see X but he seems far away and untouchable. Then later he is theatrically surrounded by women, and I think "they're fooled but I'm not". But all the time I know that I am dreaming. Then a voice says: "this is the same party before, after and during it", meaning, I know, that the way people look forward to it or remember it, changes it. Then the voice says "this is why we have reality, because it is only in *reality* that things can *really* change".

In this dream I tried to wake up but could not, which suggests that the "wise voice" was determined to put me into a position where I would have to listen and learn a lesson! The words I remembered seem a little garbled (I have written them down exactly as I found them in my dream diary) but they made great sense to me at the time and in the weeks and months that followed. At that time I certainly had a tendency to live in my imagination, to indulge in daydream and speculation at every opportunity. By using the party as an illustration, the "wise voice" seemed to be trying to show me the advantages of living in the "real" world, where actions have consequences and change is therefore possible, rather than in the dream-world where all possibilities and outcomes can be tried out and played with and nothing lasts. In fact, the message made a great impact on me: although I am interested in dreams, since *that* dream I have tried to pay as much attention as possible to my waking life and to use dreams to live it better, rather than to escape from it into the feckless pleasures of fantasy.

As for the tricky question of where the "wise voice" comes from, I am not sure – possibly from some source of "higher" knowledge within us which is normally not accessible to consciousness but becomes available in certain special circumstances – maybe when we need it, maybe when we are trying earnestly to sort ourselves out. I think it is important to distinguish this sort of voice, which firmly but gently explains or guides, from the dissociated voices which some mentally disturbed people hear, which speak obscenities or give them "instructions" which are often incompatible with the person's basic morality. A "wise voice" will never bully or coerce, and its authority comes only from our own ability to discern what is truly wise. If we do not possess the rudiments of wisdom already, it is doubtful whether a "wise voice" will speak to us, because it would be wasting its time!

It is clear that lucid dreaming represents a stage of dream-work which has immense possibilities for the extension of consciousness. If you are curious as to what those possibilities might be, Carlos Castaneda's books are a mine of fascinating ideas and techniques. Castaneda is an American anthropologist who met an old "sorcerer", Don Juan, while researching for his thesis in Mexico in 1960, and eventually became his apprentice. "Sorcerer" here does not connote someone involved in the black arts, but means the kind of magician who can manipulate both ordinary and non-ordinary reality at will. Over a period of months and years Don Juan teaches Carlos to let go of his attachment to "ordinary" reality (which Don Juan calls "the tonal") and to begin to explore the "non-ordinary world" (which he calls "the nagual"). The "nagual" is the world of "dreaming", and by "dreaming," Castaneda means a kind of "out-of-the-body" experience which is very close to what we know as lucid dreaming.

The books describe many intriguing and mysterious practices which purport to develop the art of "dreaming", but it is not necessary to engage in them to know what Don Juan means by the "non-ordinary reality" of "the nagual". Most human beings glimpse it on occasion without conscious effort; only we tend to discount or censor the impressions that arise, because they do not fit in with what we expect to experience, or rather, with what we have conditioned ourselves to experience. (Or, because we dream them, we discount them as "only a dream".)

Have you ever gazed at running water in a river for minutes at a time and noticed how, as your eyes relax and change focus, shapes and patterns appear which begin to lead you down by-ways of the imagination into something quite like another world? Or have you ever stared into a fire for a long time until your normal awareness of the flames and the scene around you has receded and been replaced by strange thoughts and fancies which you cannot quite remember when you "come to"? What Don Juan is saying, via Castaneda, is that it is possible to train the mind to follow and expand these glimpses, so that the other avenues of reality which they lead to can be explored. Eventually, he claims, this "other reality", the world of "dreaming", becomes so vivid and present to the perceiver that he can enter it at will.

How do you train the mind to do these things? The answer is not simple – if it were, I suppose we would all have been playing with these "other realities" for years. But Don Juan does give Carlos some guidelines on how to get started:

Don Juan said that there were no procedures to arrive at the attention of the nagual. He only gave me pointers. Finding my hands in dreams was the first pointer; then the exercise of paying attention was elongated to finding objects, looking for specific features, such as buildings, streets and so on. From there the jump was to "dreaming" about specific places at specific times of day. The final stage was drawing "the attention of the nagual" to focus on the total self. Don Juan said the final stage was usually ushered in by a dream many of us have had at one time or another, in which one is looking at oneself sleeping in bed. By the time a sorcerer has had such a dream, his attention has been developed to such a degree that instead of waking himself up, as most of us would do in a similar situation, he turns on his heels and engages himself in activity, as if he were acting in the world of everyday life. From that moment on there is a breakage, a division of sorts in the otherwise unified personality. The result of engaging the "attention of the nagual" and developing it to the height and sophistication of our daily attention of the world was, in Don Juan's scheme, the other self, an identical being as oneself, but made in "dreaming". (72)

Of course, such esoteric skills take years of hard work and discipline to acquire, and unless you want to be a Yacqui sorcerer, you may feel it is hardly worth the effort! Also, there is something very frightening about the model of reality which Castaneda puts forward, something which challenges the very basis of our "normal" way of experiencing the world. But if you are very brave and very curious you might find someone who would teach you how to see through the veil of "ordinary reality" to what lies beyond. It would take a long time and a great deal of patience and persistence . . . I think most of us would prefer to learn to swim in the shallows of lucid dreaming before casting aside our water-wings and venturing out there into the fathomless depths!

So, because I think that, above all, lucid dreaming should be an *enjoyable* experience, I would like to end on a humorous note, with an account which illustrates perfectly the fascinating but *infuriating* quality which pervades so many such dreams: you feel you are about to break the code, see the secrets of the universe revealed, but in fact end up more baffled than when you started!

Jane Roberts, author of the "Seth" books, had the following dream one morning after lying down to try a "dream-projection": she felt herself leave her body and travel "through the air so quickly that everything was a blur". She found herself in a strange city and wandered around exploring until she came upon a bookshop where three books by herself, on ESP, were on show. The only problem was that she knew she had not written them yet!

Startled, I looked around again. Everything seemed normal enough. Wherever I was it was a physical place. Something made me look up. A young man was looking at me with a pleased cat-caught-the-canary grin. He was one of the clerks . . .

"Uh, I haven't seen these books before," I said.

"I should think not. Where you live, you haven't written them yet," the young man said. With this he started laughing, but in a friendly open manner, as did the others who now gathered round.

"Where am I?" I asked.

He told me and said, "But forget it, that is, you won't remember anyhow."

"Oh, yes I will. I've trained myself."

"You just aren't that good at it yet," one of them said. And I really got angry. Whether I was astral-travelling or whatever, these people were having a good laugh at my expense.

"Look," I said, "I'm in my astral body. My physical body is at home in bed."

"We know that," the young man said.

The books caught my eye again. "Go ahead," he said, "memorize the titles. I'm sorry, but it won't do you any good. You won't remember." (73)

Lucid dreaming does not provide many firm answers, but it certainly raises a whole lot of new questions!

Chapter 7

True Dreaming

If you would know the invisible, seek first the visible. (74)

The vast majority of our dreams are self-centred. They are about ourselves, our wishes, fears, longings and conflicts, and the work we do on them will directly benefit *us*. These dreams may very well contain "truth", but it will be the kind of truth which tells us what we really feel about X, what is at the bottom of our reluctance to marry Y, or, more simply, that we are suffering from sexual frustration, boredom or buried grief. When we decide to do dreamwork we turn round resolutely to face these "truths" and try to deal with them constructively. The dreams have given us information about the state of our world, our own psychological back-garden, not about the big wide world outside the garden gates.

But there is another category of dreams, dreams in which we experience something which turns out to be "true" in an objective sense. I am talking about dreams with a clairvoyant, telepathic or precognitive element in them. These can be extremely trivial or profoundly significant (they have been known to save or change lives!) but always there is access to information about events in the real world of which the waking mind has no inkling. Dream books often give pages of fascinating examples of this kind of dream and their authors devise ingenious theories to explain how they come about, but the truth is that, as yet, they are a perplexing and unexplained phenomenon. However, as committed dream-workers we cannot allow ourselves simply to gape in amazement, or to turn away in scepticism: we have to attempt to make some sense of this sort of dreaming, to take an active and investigative attitude towards it. Let's start by looking at some examples of "precognitive" dreaming.

The first is a dream quoted by J.B. Priestley in his book (required reading for dream-workers!) *Man and Time*. It came from a "friendly oldish woman", who said that it was dreamed forty years ago by her younger brother. He was at that time a healthy young man of twenty-four who played football in the local team. At breakfast one morning he told his sister of a vivid dream he had just had: he was watching a funeral cortege passing down the streets near his home. The bearers wore red and white flowers in their buttonholes and his sister had on a wide black hat. He himself was following the cortege but no-one took any notice of him. His sister ribbed him about the dream and neither of them took it seriously, but three weeks later this healthy lad received a nasty kick on the football field and died of peritonitis. His funeral was exactly as he had dreamed it – the bearers wore red and white flowers (the colours of his football club), his sister wore the wide black hat, and the procession moved down just those streets he had seen in his dream. (75)

My second example comes from the poet and novelist D.M. Thomas, and it is more than a straightforward precognitive dream: Thomas dreamed that the girl at the ticket counter at Paddington station told him that he had missed the last train to Woking, and then suggested that, since she too had to get to Woking, they should share a taxi. Soon they found themselves walking down New College Lane in Oxford, looking for one. They had a pleasant conversation in which the girl told him she was an artist and he told her he was researching a thesis on Pushkin, but was really a poet. She mentioned that she loved literature, particularly Thomas Hardy. He thought what a nice intelligent girl she was. The dream ended.

Shortly afterwards, while he was in Oxford, inspiration struck: he received the germ of the idea which was to become his fine novel *The White Hotel*. Very excited, he started work on the book, breaking off after a few days to travel to London to give a poetry reading. Sitting opposite him on the train were two American girls giggling over a book on dream interpretation. One of the girls fell asleep and Thomas chatted to the other. She turned out to be an art student, but her main interest was poetry, particularly Yeats. Thomas explained that he was writing a thesis on Pushkin, but that he was really a poet himself. . . . The girl impressed him with her intelligence and attractiveness.

As soon as he got off the train, he remembered his dream: the conversation with the girl had been almost identical to the dream-conversation, with Yeats substituted for Hardy. But Yeats and Hardy were both favourites of his, and it was especially fitting that the girls had been reading a dream book when he first saw them.

This dream was "true" in more than a simple precognitive sense. Thomas wrote of it:

a poem or a novel must depend upon a happy "marriage" being achieved between the author's logical, masculine self and his feminine unconscious. My dream was predicting the onset of "The White Hotel", a novel which incidentally begins with an amorous encounter on a train. (76)

Before we start speculating and theorising about precognitive dreams, let's look at some of the problems involved in knowing whether they are genuinely precognitive or not. If we take the first dream I quoted, in which the young man apparently dreamed of his own funeral, we can easily believe that the real facts were not so clear-cut. After all, his sister was remembering something that happened forty years ago: could it not be that her brother had a much vaguer dream, which *did* perhaps have something about a funeral in it, and that the woman remembered the dream after his death and embroidered it with extra "precognitive" details to make it tally with the actual event? She would not do this consciously, of course, and her unconscious motivation might be to give meaning and dignity to her brother's tragic early death by making him "foresee" it. She would eventually be utterly convinced that the details she had invented had been there in the original. This is the phenomenon of "reading back", which sceptics often produce to scotch the idea of precognitive dreams.

Now I have to be honest and give an example of "reading back" from my own experience which proves that it is a very real danger. In my first draft of this chapter I included a dream which a schoolfriend of mine dreamed while we were in the sixth form together. As I remembered it, she dreamed that three boys from the local boys' school were involved in a car accident in the Addington Road, and that one of them was killed. The car-crash did actually happen, a few weeks later, in Addington, and, although the boys were not exactly the same three my friend had seen in her dream, they were from the same school and one of them was killed. Enough anyway to make a good example of precognitive dreaming. However, when I checked the facts with my friend, I found that she remembered the dream very differently! In her version *she* was in the car, with two boys from the school, and the crash happened in the *Selsdon* not the *Addington* Road. No-one was killed, but someone (either herself or one of the boys) got a badly crushed leg. (In the real accident one of the boys did suffer a crushed leg.)

In fact, I think the dream can still be classed as precognitive, if we believe my friend's version. But of course her version may be inaccurate too. Her memory of the original may have been distorted by time. All that we can be sure of is that, at the time when the tragic event happened, we *thought* her dream had foretold it.

The above is very typical of the kind of confusion and complication surrounding precognitive dreams. They are almost always "contaminated" by the emotional clutter of the mind which dreams them, so that the "truth" of the precognition is weakened or distorted in the smeary mirror of the individual psyche. For instance, my friend may have hung onto the detail of the crushed leg so strongly because the boy who suffered it later became a boyfriend of mine and spent a long time in hospital having his leg fixed. My friend also spent quite some time in hospital in her late adolescence. Was she identifying with the wounded boy? The fact that she thought it might have been herself who was wounded in the leg in the dream suggests that this might well be the case. And doubtless I constructed my rather convincing version of the dream as precognitive because I was writing about precognitive dreaming and needed a good example!

So, if you are interested in dreams which tell the future, you must keep an accurate diary, so that you can check up on yourself and make sure you are not "reading back" and unconsciously "improving" on the original to make it fit the facts.

It would be easy to spend the rest of this chapter giving astonishing examples of dreams which seemed to foretell the future, but it is more productive to ask who has done work on this sort of dreaming and what did they discover. One of the most influential thinkers in this area was an aeronautical engineer, J.W. Dunne, who reported on his experiments in several books, the most famous being *An Experiment with Time*. Dunne became intrigued by the topic after he noticed that several of his dreams contained material which seemed to come from the future. This was the most striking: he dreamed he was standing on high ground on an island which was in imminent peril from a volcano. He saw vapour spouting from the ground, and was seized with a frantic desire to try to save the 4,000 inhabitants of the island. The dream turned into a nightmare in which he was rushing around trying to convince the French authorities on a neighbouring island to despatch vessels to save the people on the threatened island. All through the dream the number of people – 4,000 – who needed to be saved haunted him.

A few days later a batch of newspapers arrived (Dunne was encamped with the army in a remote place which received newspapers only every few days) and in the *Daily Telegraph* he saw the headline "VOLCANO DISASTER IN MARTINIQUE . . . PROBABLE LOSS OF OVER 40,000 LIVES". The story described a volcano disaster very similar in content to the event he had dreamed. But he noted an interesting point: when he first read the headline he presumed that the number of people supposed dead was 4,000, as in his dream, not 40,000 as was actually stated in the headline, and it was only years later, when checking on the facts, that he realised what the true figure was. Furthermore, when the actual number of dead was ascertained, it turned out to be much fewer than 40,000, and the figure had no "4"s in it. Which means that what his dream foresaw was not the actual incident but his own experience of reading about it in the paper! But here the real complication enters in: did he read 4,000 instead of 40,000 because he had dreamed the figure of 4,000 first? Or did he dream 4,000 because he had a precognition of mis-reading the figure in the newspaper? He himself spotted this problem and considered it carefully: he even wondered whether he was suffering from what he called "Identifying Paramnesia", meaning that he might have invented a false memory of the dream after having read the newspaper report. (77)

At any rate, Dunne was a scientist and a rigorous thinker, so he was very anxious to get to the bottom of this strange phenomenon. He continued to observe his own dreams, and to take an interest in other people's, and eventually came to the conclusion that "dreams in general, all dreams, everybody's dreams are composed of images of past experience and images of future experience blended together in approximately equal proportions". Or rather, he strongly suspected that this might be the case and set up an experiment to test the hypothesis. He and a handful of friends made great efforts to remember their dreams over a period of time. They took particular care to write down details, especially unusual details. Then they re-read their dreams every night to see whether any image from their lives after the dream had been present in the dream. This did not happen with astounding frequency, but the fact that it happened *at all* was astonishing enough.

One of the problems in carrying out the experiment was that, before people had any chance of noticing images from the future in their dreams, they had to overcome an entirely natural resistance to the whole idea. So they used little tricks such as pretending to themselves, when they re-read their dreams, that the dream was one they were *about* to have rather than one they had had already. This helped them spot future material which they would otherwise have overlooked, thinking that it "couldn't be there". And Dunne warns that anyone wanting to try the experiment will have to follow his instructions precisely or he will have no success in overcoming the "impossibility factor".

I have found this to be true. If you expect the Dunne effect to turn up in your dreams without your looking for it, you will probably be disappointed, but if you follow his instructions carefully and use the suggested tricks, you may well come across material from the future creeping in, in just the same sly, disguised form as material from the past does. I have noticed the effect in my own dreams twice, and both times I was keeping an eye open for "forward-remembering". The clearest example is this: I dreamed I went into a shop and saw a flat mask of a clown's face on the counter. I was obliged to buy it, though I did not want it because it was so clumsily executed. The dream yielded a psychological meaning, which I duly noted, but I was puzzled as to where the image of this bizarre flat sculpture could have come from.

Two days later I was directing a cookery demonstration for a television programme. Our guest cook was a famous comic who decided on the day (I have checked with the producer that we had no advance warning) to make a clown-face salad, the kind of thing you might make for children to persuade them to eat what is good for them. It was only when I saw the image on the monitor that I recognised the flat clown-sculpture of my dream.

Of course, being an engineer and an inventor, J.W. Dunne had to invent a theory to explain why dreams used as material, things which had not yet happened. He suggested that there are at least two sorts of time: time 1, which is our normal time, and time 2, or serial time, against which we measure the flow of time 1. Beyond these two there may be an infinite series of "times", each relative to the time before and the time after. Simply, Dunne's theory is that we have a kind of "soul" which has its being in another dimension of time, from where it watches the part of ourselves which lives in normal time. This soul can therefore feed our dreams with material from the future as well as from the past.

J.B. Priestley developed this theory further: he suggested that there must be *three* levels of self, each with a different level of time to live in: self 1, the ordinary self who lives in ordinary time; self 2, a more awakened self who lives in "contemplative time"; and self 3 who is somewhat detached from the world and lives in what we might call "creative time" (because a small move made in that time can have an enormous effect at the level of ordinary time).

The next question we need to ask is: if some part of our consciousness (self 2 or self 3?) can see the future, does that mean that the future is set for us, or can we change it if we want? J.B. Priestley quotes a dream in *Man and Time* which seems to suggest that we *can* change it. A young woman dreamed that she was camping with some friends in a picturesque glade on the shores of a sound. She had some washing to do for her baby and so she took the baby and the clothes down to a little beach on the creek. She realised that she had forgotten the soap and at the same moment noticed the toddler picking up a handful of pebbles and throwing them into the water. She went for the soap but when she got back to the beach the baby was face down in the water. When she pulled him out he was dead. She woke up sobbing but was filled with joy and relief when she realised what had happened was "only a dream".

Later that summer she did go camping with some friends in a pretty glade near a creek and she did go down to the beach with the baby to do some washing. She did forget the soap, and, as she turned back to fetch it, noticed the toddler throwing pebbles into the water. The dream flashed into her mind – the child stood with his yellow curls, laughing just as he had done in the dream. Naturally enough she did not leave him there but scooped him up and ran back to her friends to tell them the story. They just laughed at her and said she had imagined it all. (78)

Looking at it subjectively and not scientifically, it seems that there is a part of us which is "in" time, and another part which is "outside" or "beyond" time. If the "outside-time" part communicates information about the future to the "inside-time" part, it is then possible for the "inside-time" part to make use of that information to influence the future, possibly in such a way that the future seen by the "outside-time" part does not actually happen. In that case, what the "outside-time" part saw was only a possible or probable future.

On the other hand, if what the "outside-time" part shows the "inside-time" part is not of any great significance (like the clown-face sculpture in my dream), then the information may not be important enough to move the "inside-time" self to act differently and change the future. In that case, the dream is indeed foretelling the future. This might explain why so many precognitive dreams have such trivial subject matter – they come true because there is no reason for them not to!

I personally do not believe that the future is set, but I do believe that we set it. Let me explain this paradoxical opinion. Most of us, by the time we have reached maturity, are very "set" in our ways. Not only do we live by a habitual pattern (we know what is good and bad, what is right and wrong, what is boring and interesting) but we think by one too: there are many concepts and possibilities which we will not allow to enter into our minds. In other words, we pay the price for security and stability, which is that we live on "automatic". We *ourselves* narrow down our range of options, so that our choice of future is very small. Is it any wonder that our lives seem so predictable?

But if we want to have an open future, we have it in our power to widen our range of options, to bring some freedom into our lives, and dreams and other precognitive glimpses can help us to do that. If we view these glimpses not as certainties but as *possibilities*, we can make an active response to them, we can ask: Do I want that to happen? If not, what can I do to stop it happening? What would I like to happen instead?

Here is an example from a friend of mine, an intelligent but rather shy woman of thirty. She was contemplating a move to London from the north and dreamed that she was in the big city and had wandered down into the underground. A group of thugs cornered her and started kicking and beating her up. Her last thought in the dream was that she was dying.

She said that this dream so alarmed her that she decided not to go to London. That may have been a sensible decision, given that she is a slightly anxious person with some health problems. On the other hand, if she had read the dream not as telling her what *would* happen to her (literally or psychologically) but as telling her what *she felt* about the idea of London, then she would have learned how frightened she was of the place and she could have asked herself why and examined the sorts of fantasies she had about it in an objective way. For instance, why was she seeing herself in a passive, victimised role? Why didn't she run, shout, protest, fight, when she was attacked by these bullies from her own unconscious? For that matter, what part of herself was bullying and threatening her?

In fact, what she did was take the dream as a confirmation of the inevitability of her passive attitude. She stayed in the north and said "No" to the risk, the adventure of London. I am not saying she was wrong to do so, because she is an imaginative person who probably prefers inner to outer adventuring; but to explore her dream before taking the decision would have given her some insight into her own emotional habits and, had she taken that insight to heart, she would have had more real freedom of choice over her course of action.

This story illustrates the point that it is wise, when attempting to understand a dream which may be clairvoyant or precognitive, to look first at your own subjective wishes, fears and fantasies. Always check that the dream is not simply giving you information about what you really feel (about a situation or a person or an idea), before you consider the precognitive possibility. This is particularly true of dreams about death; they are much more likely to be symbolic than prophetic. And even if you feel convinced that a dream could be foretelling the future, remember that the future is not absolutely "set". There is always the possibility of acting to change what happens.

That said, it would be wrong to deny that dreams do sometimes contain warnings which should be heeded, as proved by the dream quoted earlier of the woman who saw her baby drowning. If you dream that an aeroplane crashes into the Atlantic Ocean, and your husband is planning to take the early-morning flight to New York, you might well try to persuade him to put off his trip. On the other hand, dream intuitions can be "true" but irrelevant, because you cannot live someone else's life for him. I dreamed once that my oldest friend was walking a tightrope when she slipped and fell. I had to hang onto her and pull her back onto the wire. I was worried about her anyway because she had just miscarried a much-wanted child, so I rang her up to say "Look after yourself and for goodness sake don't go rushing into getting pregnant again!" But before I could speak she told me that another baby was on the way. In fact, she had a difficult pregnancy and confinement, and the child, though fine and healthy, kept her awake at night for years and exhausted her utterly. But she was prepared to pay the price to have him, and that was her decision, not mine.

In truth, the steady observation of your own dreams is the best guide in this area. You will eventually be able to discern when you are "true dreaming" and when not, and also to work out what sort of truth it is you are discerning in your dream. Again I have to say that dreams do not solve life's problems, they merely offer some insight into them. However, dream-work can build up in us the imaginative power and control to take the right action, as well as developing in us the taste for truth rather than illusion.

"True dreaming" also covers the phenomena of telepathic and clairvoyant dreams, but I do not want to give much space to these sorts of dreams because, as far as dream-work goes, there is not a great deal to be done with them except to record them carefully and speculate on how and why they happen. But they deserve a glance. Let us take telepathy first and look at examples of dreams which seem to involve the sending of a message from one mind to another.

Novelist Rider Haggard relates how he once had a dream

that his black retriever was lying on its side among brushwood and seemed to be struggling hard to communicate with him, to let him know that he (the dog) was dying. Then Haggard felt that he actually became the animal and experienced the sensation of drowning. He told the dream to his wife on waking and later found that the dog had been struck by a passing train, and after lying for some time by the railway line, had been thrown into some nearby water to drown. (79)

The second example is from my own life: I was on holiday in France while my friend, Annie, was on a meditation course in Buxton. I dreamed twice of Annie while I was away: in the first dream she had left the course early, saying it was all too much and she was fed up with it. In the second I was with her on the course and we were both very angry with a small, dark-haired man who was bullying us and pushing us around. When I got home Annie told me that she had indeed found the course "a bit too much" and had come very close to giving it up and coming home. Also she had become very angry with the man who was running the course, who was small and dark-haired . . .

In nearly all cases, telepathic dreaming seems to go on between people who have a strong emotional or spiritual connection with each other – which is not very surprising. And it is interesting that laboratory experiments on telepathic dreaming produce inconclusive results – maybe this is a phenomenon which depends upon a very particular state of mind for its success. From the two examples I have quoted, one might conclude that the sender must (consciously or unconsciously) put a great amount of emotional intensity into the message (which might be difficult to "turn on" in an experiment), and that the receiver must be in a relaxed and open state of mind.

In a full-blown clairvoyant dream, the dreamer "clearly sees" what is happening elsewhere, or else gains access to information not available to him in waking life. In *The*

Dream Game Ann Faraday describes the dream of a friend who

saw her husband placing a gold necklace around the neck of a slim, dark girl . . . it later transpired that her husband had indeed been having an affair with a girl of this description at the time, and that on the very night Elaine dreamed of the gold necklace he had given her one for her birthday that corresponded in detail with Elaine's recorded description of the dream necklace.

Ann Faraday comments that "this seemed like a genuine case of ESP being used like psychic radar to spy on her husband". (80)

How on earth did this woman manage to spy on her husband at a distance? He may well have been sending out waves of emotional intensity when he gave his mistress the necklace, but one would presume the waves were directed at his mistress not his wife! On the other hand, there must have been a strong emotional bond between husband and wife too – possibly it is not that easy to control where those waves end up! But this dream is remarkable for its visual detail – Elaine did not just have an impression of the scene, she saw the detail of the necklace. Of course, if we believe that the dreaming body can travel not just in the dream-world but in the real world, our problem is solved: Elaine was drawn to the scene by the emotional bond between herself and her husband, possibly strengthened on her part by anxiety and suspicion, and on his by guilt, and once there, she saw with the eyes of her astral form exactly what was taking place.

Well, this may or may not be the case: the rule for dream-workers is to investigate actively and to speculate by all means but not to come down too firmly for one theory or another. If you do that, you may warp later experiences to fit your theory. On the other hand, if you don't think about these matters, you won't be able to build up a framework within which to work. A framework is only provisional, but a good one, based on observation and experience, is very helpful in organising the mind and introducing some clarity into the confusing and enigmatic world of dreams.

And this brings us to the question of prophetic dreams, the kind of dreams which show forth the fate of races or nations and have little or no bearing on the personal life of the dreamer.

Here is one of the most famous prophetic dreams of all, dreamed by Pharoah, recounted in the book of Genesis, and interpreted by Joseph:

1) And it came to pass at the end of two full years, that Pharoah dreamed: and behold he stood by a river.
2) And, behold, there came up out of the river seven well favoured kine and fatfleshed; and they fed in a meadow.
3) And behold, seven other kine came up after them out of the river, ill favoured and leanfleshed; and stood by the [other] kine upon the brink of the river.
4) And the ill favoured and leanfleshed kine did eat up the seven well favoured and fat kine. So Pharoah awoke.
5) And he slept and dreamed the second time: and, behold, seven ears of corn came up upon one stalk, rank and good.
6) And, behold, seven thin ears and blasted with the east wind sprung up after them.
7) And the seven thin ears devoured the seven rank and full ears. And Pharoah awoke, and behold [it was] a dream. (81)

Having heard that Joseph had correctly interpreted dreams for a butler and a baker, Pharoah called him in and asked him to interpret these dreams. Joseph said that both dreams told the same story: Egypt was in for seven years of plenty followed by seven years of famine, and he offered to take charge of a programme to store food during the years of plenty so that there would be food enough to see them through the lean years. The Pharoah accepted and Joseph went on from strength to strength, saving the Egyptians from starvation and eventually leading his own people out of slavery towards the promised land.

Of course, it is possible that the story is true only in a mythic and not a literal sense, but that does not matter – it makes a true point either way: Joseph was obviously a canny, wise and far-seeing man. Dream interpretation was probably the least of his gifts, but it was a much respected talent in Egypt, and no doubt he saw that it could bring him power. He not only "saw" the meaning of Pharoah's prophetic dream, he also "saw" that Egypt was not organised to cope with a coming famine, and that if he could step in and become the organiser of a saving plan, then he would reap great rewards, maybe even his freedom and the freedom of his people. What I am trying to say is that true prophetic dreams come only to true prophets, whether they have the dreams or interpret them for others, and prophets are highly developed individuals who understand how the world works, can read the hearts of men and know how to act effectively and correctly in the moment of crisis. It is because their minds are already so organised and developed that they can perceive higher levels of truth than are perceptible to us ordinary mortals with our chaotic and unstable ways of thinking.

A more recent example of prophetic dreaming can be found in the experience of C.G. Jung. In the autumn of 1913, he was visited by this vision:

I saw a monstrous flood covering all the northern and low-lying lands between the north sea and the Alps. When it came up to Switzerland I saw that the mountains grew higher and higher to protect our country. I realised that a frightful catastrophe was in progress. I saw the mighty yellow waves, the floating rubble of civilisation, and the drowned bodies of uncounted thousands. Then the whole sea turned to blood. The vision lasted about one hour. I was perplexed and nauseated, and ashamed of my weakness. (82)

This vision recurred and other dreams came too:

. . . in the spring and early summer of 1914 I had a thrice-repeated dream that in the middle of summer an Arctic cold wave descended and froze the land to ice. . . . All living things were killed by frost. (83)

But the third time he had this dream of the great freeze, he saw a leaf-bearing tree among the ice, whose leaves had been transformed by the frost into "sweet grapes full of healing juices". Jung plucked the grapes and gave them to the waiting crowd.

On 1 August of that year the First World War broke out. It seemed to Jung that this was the disaster his dreams and visions had foreseen. And the ray of hope which had entered the last dream, in the shape of the grape-bearing tree, seemed to predict what Jung's own personal role in the turbulent twentieth century would be: to find and bring back a kind of knowledge which would help heal the psyche of Western man after the trauma of the war. This was the personal meaning Jung took from the dream, and almost immediately he started his journey into the depths of the unconscious, the journey which was to threaten his sanity but also provide him with material for a lifetime's work. (You can read about it in Chapter Six of *Memories, Dreams, Reflections*.)

This kind of prophetic dreaming is of a different order from ordinary precognitive dreaming: to witness the near-destruction of a civilisation is very different from dreaming of the fate of schoolboys in a car-crash. And yet, in both cases, there was a shift in consciousness to a place in which there is no past, present or future, only a "spacious present" within which past, present and possible futures can all exist.

The phrase "spacious present" comes from Maurice Nicholl, who claims in his book *Living Time* (84) that this "spacious present" is the natural habitat of man when in a heightened state of consciousness. He writes that "a change in the time sense characterises higher degrees of consciousness". Most of us have experienced these "heightened states" at some time, albeit fleetingly; it could have been the way the world slowed down and everything was seen with supernatural clarity at the moment your car slewed off the road and into a wall; it could have been the sense of meaning experienced at the bedside of someone dying; it could be a happening during meditation; it could come in a special sort of dream (see Chapter 8). However, we cannot sustain this sort of state – it fades and disappears, leaving us with a vague memory of clarity or glory which our present mind does not quite believe in.

In dreams the familiar dimensions of space are shut off from us and we are thrust into the inner space of the other dimensions – into the "spacious present" if you like. Going back to Priestley's idea of the three selves or observers of time (self 1 in normal time, self 2 in contemplative or still time, and self 3 in creative time), we see that self 1 is asleep while dreaming is happening, so that self 2, unguided by self 1's practical skills, finds he has a few problems within this "spacious present"! For instance, he cannot attend or concentrate for any length of time; as Priestley put it, "his four-dimensional focus is all at sea . . . [he is] bobbing here and there along time 1 making nonsense of his experience". (85) This is a pretty accurate description of the time and space confusion that characterises most dreams.

J.W. Dunne thought that the world of self 2 was not only the world of dreams, but also the after-death world, in which our consciousness would find itself when self 1 had passed away for good. He notes that, in self 2's world, the self is able to blend together two or more impressions which are separated in time 1, and he suggests that, in our time 2 after-life, we will learn how to combine all the elements of our time 1 existence into new events and meanings, just as an artist might take various sketches from his notebooks and combine them on his final canvas into a finished work.

This is a delightful and ingenious idea, but maybe we do not have to wait until we are dead to set about learning how to live in the dream-world and become effective there. The kind of conscious dream-work suggested in this book begins the education of the dreaming body who lives in time 2, while we are still alive! On the other hand, let's be careful not to become too carried away! We are in this present physical world for a reason: we must not let ourselves slide into thinking of the dream-world as somehow superior to it. Again, J.W. Dunne has an intriguing theory which fits in here: he believed that self 1, with his sharp focus in time 1, is *educating* self 2. If this is true, then the best way we can help in this educative process is to make self 1's focus in this world as sharp as possible – in other words, "if you would know the invisible, seek first the visible". And there is not much point in undertaking any of the higher stages of dream-work until we have done a great deal of work on our waking selves, developing and cleansing our powers of observation and discrimination, and sorting out our psychological tangles.

In fact, Dunne's theory is really only a refinement of the old, old notion that we each have an immortal soul whose fate depends upon what we do while incarnated on this earth. But it is none the worse for that. Obviously those of us who are interested in self-development hope that this "development" does not stop with death. We may be wrong, but my guess is that we live more fully and bravely in this hope than without it. At any rate, I have to say at this point that if your interest in dream-work is more than a passing one, and if you have benefited from it, you will probably find at some stage that you have to make a choice about which direction to follow, because, in this "time", we cannot follow all directions at once!

You may decide to stick with the psychological level of dream-work, running groups or working with people interested in the therapeutic use of dreams. Or you may find that dream-work has opened up new avenues of creativity for you and want to explore those avenues rather than the dreams which pointed the way. However, if you follow instead the line of self-development via dreams, if you become a committed explorer of the unknown worlds within, then you will probably find that dream-work makes you curious about other methods which have been evolved for exploring the unknown. I cannot tell you what the right ones would be for you – you may find that the insight dream-work affords will enable you to see what lies behind the symbolic languages of the great religions and you may find that within Christianity or Buddhism there is a path mapped out for you. Or you may be drawn towards the simplicity and discipline of a meditation practice. Or you may find a philosophical study group which offers you the chance to explore in more depth some of the themes touched on in this book. It really depends what kind of person you are in essence. But whatever path you take, the test of its value is whether it makes you more alive and more aware in the waking world as well as in the dream-world.

I have mentioned at various points throughout this book the dangers of withdrawing from the real world into a private dream-world in which you need not be touched or challenged by the demands of our common reality. True developmental work is always a struggle, because it demands that we face what we are, what is real. It is naturally much easier to live inside a cocoon spun from desires and delusions. Dream-work can lead to self-obsession, to a strengthening of the walls of the cocoon; or it can lead to objectivity and clarity, to an understanding of how those walls are made and how to break them down.

I shall not end this chapter with a quotation from a book of ancient wisdom, but with a few lines from our old friend Seth, the discarnate entity.

I am an individual. I form my physical environment. I change and make my world. I am free of space and time. I am a part of all that is. There is no place within me that creativity does not exist. (86)

And I would like to add, to reinforce my point, that when I finish writing the first draft of this book I shall be going off to earn my living making a film for a television company about the dangers of hazardous chemicals. If I cannot bring to bear on this hard-edged, down-to-earth film any of the skills I have learnt from dream-work (like clarity, concentration, Active Imagination), then it will be a poor show. But I shall not find it easy out there in the "real" world . . . it is so tempting to linger on here in the magical world of dreams.

Chapter 8

"Big" Dreams

A star was broken and out poured showers of light . . . (87)

"Big" dreams come to us very rarely, but when they do, they can change our lives. They cannot be produced by "work", neither do they need to be "worked" on afterwards. They come by grace (or by accident, if you are an atheist) and their meaning is always clear – the intellect may not be able to abstract that meaning, but the heart is touched, the foundations are shaken, or the dreamer is moved in some perhaps not easily definable way. The voice of the Real has spoken, and all the dreamer is required to do is to sit still and pay attention. The dream may point a direction, impart knowledge or simply afford a glimpse of another world where everything is rich and strange. You wake from these dreams with a sense of awe, of privilege, of a gift given and received. And, most interestingly of all, you may know very well at the time that you are dreaming, *but it does not matter*, because the truth of the dream is so vivid, so convincing that it makes the customary distinction between the "real world" and the "dream world" seem irrelevant.

These dreams seem to come from a higher reality, a reality more highly charged and numinous than our usual waking or dreaming realities. They represent a purification and clarification of the dreaming process, a proof of the depth and extraordinary richness of mind, a depth from which we are normally cut off. And although I would guess that most of us have one or two "big" dreams in the course of our lives, they are certainly more common in people of a high level of psychological and/or spiritual organisation, people like Jung, St Theresa of Avila, Emanuel Swedenborg, or the indefatigable J.W. Dunne.

I do not want to theorise about this sort of dreaming, but rather to give you a taste of its moods and qualities. Let us start with Dunne, the engineer who combined the rigours of a scientific approach with the openness and enthusiasm of an artist in dealing with his own and others' dreams. By the time he had the following dream, he was very much at home in the dream-world, and he states that he knew he was dreaming and that he also knew perfectly well that the dream was an *allegory*. It came at a time when he was wrestling with ambivalent feelings about the Christian idea of God. (I have had to shorten and paraphrase it because Dunne is delightfully long-winded in his own account.)

He dreamed he was sitting on a hillside in bright sunlight and saw footprints leading up to the edge of a brook. He knew that they were his own footprints, that the brook was Jordan, and that he was dead. On the other side of the brook the world he had left lay in deep shadow. Then he noticed that, a hundred yards to the left (the detail is typical of Dunne), God was sitting working with bent head. Dunne could not actually see Him properly because he could not turn his head, but he knew that He was there.

There was an angelic being nearby whom Dunne consciously clothed in traditional Angel raiment before asking him why men in the world did not see God's shadow. "It's everywhere," he continued. "It's all around them! Why, why don't they see it?"

"Because it has no edges," the Angel replied.

Dunne then found himself "really wide awake", utterly convinced by the Angel's answer. It satisfied him completely. He wrote: "It is logically impossible to be aware of anything which has no edges." (88)

Some time later, after reading a depressing book which suggested that nature would probably soon toss man aside as a failed experiment, Dunne dreamed of the Angel again.

"How can I be sure that it is going to turn out all right for us [meaning the human race]?" he asked.

The Angel paused and then answered, very slowly and emphatically: "Always – remember – this: – whatever – the game – is – you – had – a hand – in – the *making* of it. . . . Is it likely – you would have made it turn out wrong for yourself?"

While the Angel spoke, Dunne found himself delightedly saying: "Yes, I see!" and joining in with the last part of the Angel's statement, so that their voices were mingled. Afterwards he wrote:

I must confess it. There had been, at that moment, no doubt in my mind. I knew that somehow, somewhere, sometime, we had all consulted together, that we had decided upon the steps to be taken, *and that I had agreed to my share of these.* And, looking at that delighted conversation in retrospect, I realise now that it was exactly *this* that I had felt in the last of those boyhood ecstasies, when I had stared out of the window towards the hidden multitude who were waiting to see if I should remember the thing I had always known. (89)

This brings us to that great spiritual dreamer, Emanuel Swedenborg, who started by recording and studying his dreams and ended by having visionary access to all the worlds of heaven and hell. The following dream illustrates, as Dunne's dreams do, the *unexpectedness* of the spiritual world. We might imagine it to be all glory and glamour, thunderous pronouncements and Holy Citadels dripping with diamond and crystal, but here Swedenborg dreams of Jesus as a friend:

It seemed as if it were Christ Himself, with whom I associated as with another person, without ceremony. He borrowed a little money from another person, about five pounds. I was vexed because he did not borrow it from me. I took up two pounds, but it seemed to me that I dropped one of them, and likewise the other one. He asked what it was. I said that I had found two and that one of them might have been dropped by Him. I handed them over, and He accepted. In such an innocent manner we seemed to live together, which was a state of innocence. (90)

Through his deep investigations of the world of dream and the world of spirit, Swedenborg brought back many ideas fascinating to dream-workers and, indeed, many of his explanations and descriptions remind us of the extra dimensions of time about which Dunne and Priestley talked, and into which we move in dreams and in death.

However, we must be clear that "big" dreams do not always clothe themselves in religious imagery. An ordinary, intelligent young man had two unusual dreams within a short period, just before he decided to join our dream-group:

I discovered a clock. It was the most fantastic clock you can imagine. It was just superb. I just wanted to be with that clock for ever. It was the ultimate thing, the clock of clocks. That was it. If I could be with that clock that was all I wanted!

I was sitting in front of the fire . . . not exactly dreaming but intently concentrating on an image of a golden cross with a snake wound round the cross . . . it was constantly moving . . . like in the infinity sign . . . this green snake moving round and around. . . . When I came to, I realised I had been sitting there with my eyes closed concentrating on that image for a very long time.

While not quite extraordinary enough to be classed as "big", these dreams share the numinous, unanalysable quality of true "big" dreams. They spoke directly to the heart and reminded the young man of the depth and mysteriousness of life, which he had probably been overlooking in the pursuit of his career as a lawyer. His second experience, "not exactly dreaming but intently concentrating", is a good example of a phenomenon common with "big" dreams, of increased focus and clarity within a state which is not quite sleeping and not quite waking. (For this reason it is difficult to make a clear distinction between "big" dreams and visions.) We meet this strange state again in a dream quoted by Marganita Laski in her book on ecstasy. Interestingly, the woman dreamer had been a member of a dream-group and was practised in writing down her dreams as soon as she awoke.

Therefore her record is fresh and accurate, and she is obviously trying very hard to get down the essence of the experience:

This is not perhaps exactly a whole dream at all, an experience, a marvellous feeling, a state, I don't know: woke, time not known, suddenly, easily, without shock. Just awake, feeling extraordinary, marvellous, as if everything, whole answer to everything, all problems of life, were just round the corner, so near, so close, could almost touch them, the whole whatever may be: the feeling is impossible to describe. The whole was there, so near, just out of sight it is true, but that did not matter. It *was* there. As well as the impossible to describe feelings there was more concrete sight or rather sight and feeling perhaps, as if a star was suddenly broken and out poured showers of light. That does not really quite describe it either: Streams, showers of silver white light, brittle: cascading up (I know) and down (I think). As if a rock, crystal, star, some substance broke, shattered, and all these streams, lines, poured up from it (and down, not sure). Fireworks, perhaps, the nearest description, but unlike fireworks this light was white? or silver, also it was at the *side* of the dream? That sounds silly, I mean, supposing the dream a cinema screen, then the breaking light, showering light, was at the left side rather. But spread all around I think. Several times in the night I woke after this, each time I thought and felt and went over the experience, unconsciously I mean, and now, on waking, write it down. (91)

Normal punctuation and grammar go to pot as the dreamer struggles to put into words what was for her an ineffable experience.

But such dream-visions can be very simple. Once, while under a deal of pressure while making a film abroad, I was lying dozing on my hotel bed, when I "saw" a warm golden-orangey light shining out of the doorway of a room in what looked like a university courtyard. The fiery light was drawing me, welcoming me. I knew that in that room everything would be well and I would be united with my own people in the radiant warmth. I can still call up the feeling of that vision and it is still as comforting to me now as it was in the bleak moment when it appeared. But the comfort it offered was not the comfort of a snug and soothing sleep wrapped in warm blankets. Rather it had that quality of exhilarating, energising *ease* you feel when you are in the right place at the right time with the right people doing the right thing. A sense of homecoming would be the most accurate way of putting it.

In the course of his long, adventurous life, Jung (who coined the expression "big dream") had many numinous dreams. My favourite is the one set in Liverpool (one of my favourite cities). It occurred at a time when Jung was much preoccupied with ideas about the centre and the "Self", and had been painting pictures of mandalas, which he thought to be symbolic of the "Self".

I found myself in a dirty, sooty city. It was night, and winter, and dark, and raining. I was in Liverpool. With a number of Swiss . . . I walked through the dark streets. I had the feeling that we were coming up from the harbour, and that the real city was up on the cliffs. We climbed up there. . . . When we reached the plateau, we found a broad square dimly illuminated by street lights, into which many streets converged. The various quarters of the city were arranged radially round the square. In the centre was a round pool, and in the middle of it a small island. While everything around it was obscured by rain, fog, smoke, and dimly lit darkness, the little island blazed with sunlight. On it a single tree, a magnolia, in a shower of reddish blossoms. It was as though the tree stood in sunlight and was at the same time the source of the light. (92)

Jung recognised the dream as very important: the city had appeared to him as a mandala, with the radiant island at its centre. Liverpool was "the pool of life", the "liver", meaning "the seat of life". It brought to him the understanding that

one could not go beyond the centre. The centre is the goal, and everything is directed towards that centre. Through this dream I understood that the Self is the principle and archetype of orientation and meaning. Therein lies its healing function.

He wrote that "without such a vision I might perhaps have lost my orientation and been compelled to abandon my undertaking". (93) It is significant (and this is a quality you find in many "big" dreams) that although the dream *did* have a personal meaning for Jung, it is a dream which can move and inspire others too – it has an archetypal resonance, just as great novels or paintings do.

On a humbler level, there is the dream of a young medical student who was just coming to terms with his first experience in the dissecting room, a testing time for an aspiring doctor. He dreamed that he walked alone into the dissecting room and saw a corpse on a slab. He noticed the scalpel wounds in its flesh. Then, as he approached, the corpse sat up and water began to gush out of its wounds. The phrase "streams of living water" came into his head. The young man was profoundly stirred by this dream and felt that it was confirming him in his vocation as a healer.

All the great religions recognised the divine aspect of dreaming, and quite often great religious dreams take the form of an ascent into heaven. Jacob's dream of the ladder is a classic example:

And he dreamed, and behold a ladder set up on the earth, and the top of it reached to heaven; and behold the angels of God ascending and descending on it. (94)

The patriarchs and prophets had dreams in plenty, according to the Bible, but, interestingly, Jesus is not reported as being inspired or influenced by dreams – perhaps, as an entirely enlightened man, he could read God's heart without mediation of imagery. Mohammed, however, was a visionary who received the Koran from an archangelic presence who told him he was the "Messenger of God" and ordered him to "Recite!" while he, the archangel, dictated. In the course of his life as a prophet he had the famous dream which is known as "The Night Journey". The details of this are not given in the Koran, but tradition provides them in plenty.

It is said that in the middle of a still, solemn night Mohammed was awakened by a voice crying "Sleeper awake!" and before him stood the angel Gabriel in all his radiant glory, leading a fantastical steed, Boraq, who had a human face and eagle's wings. On Boraq's back the prophet flew via Mount Sinai and Bethlehem to Jerusalem, where he prayed in the ruins of the Temple of Solomon with Abraham and then saw an endless ladder appear upon Jacob's rock.

He mounted into the first heaven where he met Adam, and then into the other six heavens where he met the other prophets and finally Jesus. He saw many marvellous things including the Angel of Death, Azrael, who was so huge that his eyes were separated by 70,000 marching days! Finally, Mohammed was carried to the top of the Lotus-Tree of Heaven which flowered at the right of God's invisible throne. After travelling through regions of dazzling light and deepest darkness, through clouds and choirs of angels bowed down and motionless in complete silence, he felt himself carried into the light of his Lord. From there, heaven and earth combined appeared almost imperceptible to him, as if melted into nothingness and reduced to the size of a grain of mustard-seed in the middle of a field. Then he beheld God with the eyes of his soul, and the Almighty placed one hand on Mohammed's breast and the other on his shoulder so that, to the marrow of his bones, he felt an icy chill, followed by an inexpressible feeling of calm and ecstatic annihilation.

Before they parted, God instructed Mohammed to make his followers say fifty prayers a day, but Mohammed met Moses on the way down and Moses persuaded him that fifty prayers a day was unrealistic. Mohammed therefore returned to God and God brought the number down to five! After visiting paradise, Mohammed returned home on Boraq. (95)

Had I not encountered Swedenborg's and Dunne's dreams, I might have found the piece about bargaining with God for a reduction in the number of prayers somewhat bizarre and inappropriate, but it is just such human details which make these "big" dreams so resonant. If they were just cosmic mystery tours they would touch us much less.

Perhaps because of Mohammed's magnificent dream, dreaming has always been acknowledged within Islam's mystical tradition of Sufism as a valid way of knowledge and spiritual initiation. Shamsoddin Lahiji, who lived in the fifteenth century, reports this vision, which he had one night while absorbed in deep meditation:

I saw that the entire universe, in the structure it presents, consists of light. Everything had become one colour, and all the atoms of all the beings proclaimed "I am the Truth", each in the manner proper to its being and with the force particular to each. I was unable to interpret properly what manner of being had made them proclaim this. Having seen these things in my vision, an intoxication and an exaltation, a desire and an extraordinary delectation were born within me. I wanted to fly in the air, but I saw that there was something resembling a piece of wood at my feet which prevented my taking flight. With violent emotion, I kicked the ground in every possible manner until this piece of wood let go. Like an arrow shooting forth from the bow, but a hundred times stronger, I rose and moved into the distance. When I arrived at the first Heaven, I saw that the moon had split, and I passed through the moon. Then, returning from this state and absence, I found myself again present. (96)

It would seem that, for the great saints and mystics (if they were inclined to visionary experience in the first place, and of course not all were), there would come a time when the spiritual world would impinge so strongly into the material world that the eyes of the spirit would open and "see", right in the midst of ordinary life while the person was wide awake. St Theresa of Avila experienced this sort of waking vision for most of her devotional life, but although she was convinced of the truth and value of what she saw, her spiritual director was not, and this tormented poor Theresa to the point that she actually prayed to God to "lead me by another way". But her visions persisted and intensified, until one day, while in prayer, she had this experience:

I saw Christ close by me, or to speak more correctly, felt Him; for I saw nothing with the eyes of the body, nothing with the eyes of the soul. He seemed to me to be close beside me; and I saw too, as I believe, that it was He who was speaking to me.

She explained the sensation further:

He renders Himself present to the soul by a certain knowledge of Himself which is more clear than the sun. I do not mean that we now see either a sun or any other brightness, only that there is a light not seen, which illumines the understanding, so that the soul may have the fruition of so great a good. This vision brings with it great blessings. (97)

I have quoted Theresa's vision because I believe that, at their greatest, "big" dreams always happen when the dreamer is *awake*, but not just awake in the normal sense, *awake* in the sense of being open to a far wider and deeper range of perceptions and influences than normal. So that, in fact, it matters little whether these visions come while a person is asleep or awake, because the shift in consciousness which he or she experiences is certainly to a level *higher* than either normal sleeping or waking.

This raises many fascinating questions about the relationship of "dream" to "reality", which the Christian church has chosen largely to ignore. To explore these questions further we have to turn to the Tibetan Buddhists and their Dream Doctrine.

After many years of solitary meditation, the great Tibetan yogi, Milarepa, had won such power over his dreams that he could:

traverse the summit of Mount Meru to its base – and I saw everything clearly as I went. Likewise in my dreams I could multiply myself into hundreds of personalities, all endowed with the same powers as myself. Each of my multiplied personalities could traverse space, go to some Buddha Heaven, listen to the teachings there and then come back and teach the Dharma to many persons. I could also transform my physical body into a mass of blazing fire, or into an expanse of flowing or calm water. Seeing that I had obtained infinite phenomenal power even though it be but in my dreams, I was filled with happiness and encouragement. (98)

(If only Theresa had met Milarepa – she would not have needed to feel so guilty and anxious about her visions!)

The Dream Doctrine teaches that he who has become active and creative in the dream-world has begun to grasp the nature of illusion and solve the problem of reality. In fact, he becomes a creator, a very god in his dreams. But the next step is to go *beyond* these images to the source of them. Instructions on how to do this are given in *The Tibetan Book of the Dead*, addressed to the soul just before and after the hour of death, while it is hanging about in that place between birth and death called the "bardo". The object of all the tender and strenuous exhortations of the book is to persuade the soul to recognise that all the "peaceful or wrathful deities" it may see are simply thought-forms which it has itself created, and then to see behind them to the "Clear Light of Reality".

O nobly-born, when thy body and mind were separating, thou must have experienced a glimpse of the pure Truth, subtle, sparkling, bright, dazzling, glorious, and radiantly awesome, in appearance like a mirage moving across a landscape in spring-time in one continuous stream of vibrations. Be not daunted thereby, nor terrified, nor awed. That is the radiance of thine own true nature. Recognise it.

From the midst of that radiance, the natural sound of Reality, reverberating like a thousand thunders simultaneously sounding, will come. This is the natural sound of thine own real self. Be not daunted thereby or terrified, nor awed. (99)

This expresses in much more elevated form what I was saying in the previous chapter: that once a person has explored the world of dreams thoroughly and perhaps begun to have some power over his own dreams, he will come to a stage, where, if he is a true explorer and not a dilettante, he will want to know about the force which lies behind dreams, the force which the imagery of dreams clothes and makes present to us, whether in the humble form of a truth about our psychological world, or in an exalted intimation of the nature of heaven and earth. This is because dreams and dream-work are a means to an end, not an end in themselves. We must always look beyond the form of a dream to its meaning, and then beyond its meaning . . . to what?

I would not presume to answer that question for you because I would not wish to deprive you of the great adventure of finding out for yourself. Indeed, I could not do that even if I wanted to, because that kind of knowledge cannot be passed on directly man to man. Each individual must experience it for him or herself.

So, let me avoid the temptation to babble about cosmic truths and end this book with one of the most wonderful "big dreams" I have ever come across. It was dreamed by that generous soul, J.B. Priestley, and it is good to know that his dreams could be as wise and as thrilling as his books.

I dreamt I was standing at the top of a very high tower, alone, looking down upon myriads of birds all flying in one direction; every kind of bird was there, all the birds in the world. It was a noble sight, this vast aerial river of birds. But now in some mysterious fashion the gear was changed, and time speeded up, so that I saw generations of birds, watched them break their shells, flutter into life, weaken, falter, and die. Wings grew only to crumble; bodies were sleek and then, in a flash, bled and shrivelled; and death struck everywhere at every second. What was the use of all this blind struggle towards life, this eager trying of wings, all this gigantic meaningless biological effort? As I stared down, seeming to see every creature's ignoble little history almost at a glance, I felt sick at heart. It would be better if not one of them, not one of us at all, had been born, if the struggle ceased forever. I stood on my tower, still alone, desperately unhappy. But now the gear was changed again and time went faster still, and it was rushing by at such a rate that the birds could not show any movement but were like an enormous plain sewn with feathers. But along this plain, flickering through the bodies themselves, there now passed a sort of white flame, trembling, dancing, then hurrying on; and as soon as I saw it I knew that this flame was life itself, the very quintessence of being; and then it came to me, in a rocket-burst of ecstasy, that nothing mattered, nothing could ever matter, because nothing else was real, but this quivering and hurrying lambency of being. Birds, men, or creatures not yet shaped and coloured, all were of no account except so far as this flame of life travelled through them. It left nothing to mourn over behind it: what I had thought was tragedy was mere emptiness or a shadow show, for now all real feeling was caught and purified and danced on ecstatically with the white flame of life. I have never felt before such deep happiness as I knew at the time of my dream of the tower and the birds. (100)

NOTES

CHAPTER 1

(1) Homer: *The Odyssey*. Translated by E.V. Rieu. Penguin 1946 (1986) Book xix.

(2) Jung C.G.: *Zarathustra*. Privately circulated seminar notes, quoted by Frances G. Wickes in *The Inner World of Choice* (see 19).

CHAPTER 2

(3) Bro, Harmon H.: *Edgar Cayce on Dreams*. New York: Paperback Library 1968.

(4) Mindell, Arnold: *Dreambody*. Routledge and Kegan Paul 1982 (1984).

(5) Aristides, quoted by E.R. Dodds in *The Greeks and the Irrational*. Boston 1957.

(6) Blacker, Carmen: *The Catalpa Bow*. George Allen and Unwin Ltd 1975 (1986).

(7) Eliade, Mircea: *Shamanism: Archaic Techniques of Ecstasy*. Routledge and Kegan Paul 1964.

(8) Freud, Sigmund: *The Interpretation of Dreams*. Translated by James Strachey. Penguin (Pelican) 1976 (1986).

(9) Ibid.

(10) Ibid.

(11) Ibid.

(12) Ibid.

(13) Ibid.

(14) Jung C.G.: *The Freud/Jung Letters*. Edited by William McGuire, and abridged by Alan McGlashan. Picador 1979.

(15) Ibid.

(16) Jung C.G.: *Memories, Dreams, Reflections*. Fontana 1967 (Flamingo 1986).

(17) Horney, Karen: *Neurosis and Human Growth*. W.W. Norton and Co. (America) 1950.

(18) Ibid.

(19) Wickes, Frances G.: *The Inner World of Choice*. Coventure 1977.

CHAPTER 3

(20) Williams, Strephon Kaplan: *The Dreamwork Manual*. Aquarian 1984 (1986).

(21) Mindell, Arnold: *Working with the Dreaming Body*. Routledge and Kegan Paul 1985.

(22) Stewart, Kilton: *Dream Theory in Malaya*, from *Altered States of Consciousness*, ed. Charles Tart. John Wiley (America) 1969.

(23) Von Franz, Marie Louise: *The Process of Individuation* from *Man and his Symbols*, ed. C.G. Jung. Aldus Books 1964 (Picador 1986).

(24) Williams, Strephon Kaplan: see 20.

(25) Ibid.

(26) Mindell, Arnold: see 4.

(27) Ibid.

(28) Mindell, Arnold: see 21.

(29) Faraday Ann: *The Dream Game*. Penguin Books 1976.

(30) Ibid.

(31) Von Franz, Marie Louise: see 23.

(32) Jung, Carl Gustav: see 16.

CHAPTER 4

(33) Rumi, Jelaluddin (trans. John Moyne and Coleman Barks): *Open Secret – Versions of Rumi*. Threshold Books (America) 1984. Quatrain 91.

(34) Jung, Carl Gustav: *The Transcendent Function* in *Collected Works Vol. 8*. (The Structure and Dynamics of the Psyche) RKP 1978.

(35) Ibid.

(36) Ibid.

(37) "Seth" via Jane Roberts: *The Unknown Reality*. Prentice Hall (America) 1977.

(38) Ibid.

(39) "Seth" via Jane Roberts: *The Seth Material*. Prentice Hall (America) 1970.

(40) Chetwynd, Tom: *Dictionary for Dreamers*. Granada 1981.

CHAPTER 5

(41) Blake, William: Letter to Trusler, Aug. 23 1799, printed in *William Blake: His Philosophy and Symbol* (see 53 below).

(42) Schatzman, Morton: *Dreaming Solutions*, article in *Mathematics Teaching*, Dec. 1983.

(43) Schatzman, Morton: *Dream power solves life's puzzles*, article in *The Independent*, Dec. 23 1986.

(44) Kekulé von Stradonitz, F.G.: quoted in *Dreamers* by John Grant. Grafton 1986.

(45) Stevenson, Robert Louis: *A Chapter on Dreams* from *Across the Plains*. Chatto and Windus 1913.

(46) Ibid.

(47) Ibid.

(48) Lindop, Grevel: *The Opium Eater: a life of Thomas de Quincey*. Oxford University Press 1985.

(49) De Quincey, Thomas: *Confessions of an English Opium Eater* (1821). Penguin Classics 1986.

(50) Ibid.

(51) Ibid.

(52) Blake, William: *Jerusalem* as printed in *Blake: Complete Writings*. OUP 1966.

(53) Damon, S.F.: *William Blake: His Philosophy and Symbol* (1924). Peter Smith (America) 1958.

(54) Ibid.

(55) As 41.

(56) Ernst, Max: *Beyond Painting* in *Cahiers d'Art Paris* 1936.

(57) Breton, André: *Surrealist Manifesto* 1924, quoted in Breton's *What is Surrealism?* Faber and Faber 1936.

(58) Aragon, Louis: *Une Vague de Rêves* 1924, quoted in *Surrealists and Surrealism* by Gaetan Picon, Macmillan 1983.

(59) Breton, André: see 57.

(60) "Seth", via Jane Roberts: *The Nature of the Psyche*. Prentice Hall (America) 1979.

(61) Ibid.

(62) Stewart, Kilton: see 22.
(63) Ibid.

CHAPTER 6

(64) See 71 below.
(65) Van Eeden, Frederick: *A Study of Dreams* in *Altered States of Consciousness* (see 22).
(66) Faraday, Ann: see 29.
(67) Subject B, quoted by Celia Greene in *Lucid Dreams*. Institute of Psychophysical Research 1968 (1982).
(68) Fox, Oliver: *Astral Projection*. University Books Inc. New York 1962.
(69) Subject B: see 67.
(70) Fox, Oliver: *Astral Projection* see 68.
(71) Subject B: see 67.
(72) Castaneda, Carlos: *The Second Ring of Power*. Penguin 1979.
(73) Roberts, Jane: *The Seth Material*. Prentice Hall 1970.

CHAPTER 7

(74) Ancient Hebrew saying.
(75) Dream collected by J.B. Priestley, printed in *Man and Time*. Aldus 1964.
(76) Thomas, D.M.: *How My Dreams Come True*, article in *Cosmopolitan*, Sept. 1986.
(77) Dunne, J.W.: *An Experiment with Time*. Faber and Faber 1938 (First ed. 1927) Chapter Six.
(78) Dream quoted by J.B. Priestley in *Man and Time* (see 75).
(79) Haggard, Rider: quoted by John Grant in *Dreamers*. Grafton 1986.
(80) Faraday Ann: see 29.
(81) *Genesis* 41 verses i–vii.
(82) Jung, C.G.: see 16.
(83) Ibid.
(84) Nicholl, Maurice: *Living Time*. Vincent Stuart 1952, Shambala 1985.
(85) Priestley, J.B.: see 75.
(86) "Seth", via Jane Roberts: see 73.

CHAPTER 8

(87) See 91.
(88) Dunne, J.W.: *Intrusions*. Faber and Faber 1955.
(89) Ibid.
(90) Swedenborg, Emanuel: *Journal of Dreams* para. 276
      (Quoted in *The Presence of Other Worlds* by Wilfred Van
      Dusen. Wildwood 1975).
(91) Collected by Marganita Laski and printed in her book
      Ecstasy. The Cresset Press 1971.
(92) Jung, C.G.: see 16.
(93) Ibid.
(94) *Genesis* 28 xii.
(95) Dermengham, Emile: *The Life of Mahomet*. Routledge
      1930.
(96) Lahiji, Shamsoddin, dream quoted in *Sufi Expressions of
      The Mystic Quest* by Laleh Bakhtiar. Thames and Hudson
      1979.
(97) St Theresa: *Vida*, quoted by Evelyn Underhill in *Mysticism*.
      Methuen 1911 (1960).
(98) Evans-Wentz, W.Y. (ed.): *Tibet's Great Yogi, Milarepa*.
      O.U.P. 1928 (1974).
(99) Evans-Wentz, W.Y. (ed.): *The Tibetan Book of the Dead*.
      O.U.P. 1927 (1984).
(100) Priestley, J.B.: *Rain upon Godshill*. Heinemann 1939.

SOME SUGGESTED READING

Blacker, Carmen, *The Catalpa Bow*, George Allen and Unwin, 1982

Breton, André, *What is Surrealism?*, Faber and Faber, 1936

Castaneda, Carlos, *The Second Ring of Power* (and the other six books in the series), Penguin, 1979

Damon, S.F, *William Blake: His Philosophy and Symbol*, Peter Smith (U.S.), 1958

De Quincey, Thomas, *Confessions of an English Opium Eater*, Penguin Classics, 1986

Dunne, J.W., *An Experiment with Time*, Macmillan, 1981

Dunne, J.W., *Intrusions*, Faber and Faber, 1955

Eliade, Mircea, *Shamanism: Archaic Techniques of Ecstasy*, RKP, 1964

Evans-Wentz, W.Y. (ed.), *The Tibetan Book of the Dead*, OUP, 1984

Faraday, Ann, *The Dream Game*, Penguin, 1976

Freud, Sigmund, *The Interpretation of Dreams*, Pelican, 1976

Grant, John, *Dreamers*, Grafton, 1986

Greene, Celia, *Lucid Dreams*, Institute of Psychophysical Research, 1968 (1982)

Horney, Karen, *Neurosis and Human Growth*, Norton and Co. (U.S.), 1950

Irwin, Robert, *The Arabian Nightmare*, Dedalus, 1984

Jung, C.G., *Memories, Dreams, Reflections*, Fontana, 1967, Flamingo, 1986

Jung, C.G. (ed.), *Man and His Symbols*, Aldus Books, 1964, Picador, 1986

Jung, C.G., *Dreams*, Princeton/Bollingen, 1974

Lewis, C.S., *Voyage of the Dawntreader*, Fontana 1980 (1952)

Lindop, Grevel, *The Opium Eater: a life of Thomas de Quincey*, OUP, 1985

Mindell, Arnold, *Dreambody*, RKP, 1982

Mindell, Arnold, *Working with the Dreaming Body*, RKP, 1985

Nicholl, Maurice, *Living Time*, Shambala, 1985

Priestley, J.B., *Man and Time*, Aldus, 1964

Roberts, Jane, *The Seth Material*, Prentice Hall (U.S.), 1970
Roberts, Jane, *The Unknown Reality*, Prentice Hall, 1977
Stevenson, Robert L., *Across the Plains*, Chatto and Windus, 1913
Stewart, Kilton, *Dream Theory in Malaya* (in *Altered States of Consciousness*, John Wiley (U.S.), 1969)
Underhill, Evelyn, *Mysticism*, Methuen, 1960 (1911)
Van Dusen, Wilfred, *The Presence of Other Worlds: the findings of Emanuel Swedenborg*, Wildwood, 1975
Wickes, Frances G., *The Inner World of Choice*, Coventure, 1977
Williams, Charles, *Descent into Hell*, Eerdman's (America), 1949
Williams, Strephon Kaplan, *The Dreamwork Manual*, Aquarian, 1984

Index